VERENA STAËL VON HOLSTEIN
She studied surveying and hydrograp
programmer and in the hydrographic
homemaker with two children, and live
Heide, a heathland region in Norther
work of Rudolf Steiner, from childhood onwards she has been able to
perceive the etheric and astral realms in human beings and the natural
world. She has learnt over many years to train her metaphysical perceptions so that communication with nature spirits takes place almost
as a matter of course. She receives answers spiritually in the form of
patterns, ideas and sometimes also images, and translates them into
human concepts. She is the author of several books, including *Nature
Spirits and What They Say.*

NATURE SPIRITS OF THE TREES

AND WHAT THEY WANT TO TELL US

Messages from the Beings of the Trees

Verena Staël von Holstein

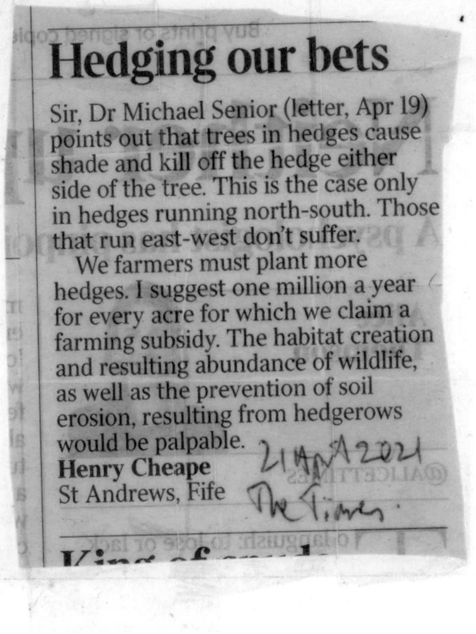

Hedging our bets

Sir, Dr Michael Senior (letter, Apr 19) points out that trees in hedges cause shade and kill off the hedge either side of the tree. This is the case only in hedges running north-south. Those that run east-west don't suffer.

We farmers must plant more hedges. I suggest one million a year for every acre for which we claim a farming subsidy. The habitat creation and resulting abundance of wildlife, as well as the prevention of soil erosion, resulting from hedgerows would be palpable.
Henry Cheape
St Andrews, Fife

21 APR 2021
The Times.

CLAIRVIEW

Clairview Books Ltd.,
Russet, Sandy Lane,
West Hoathly,
W. Sussex RH19 4QQ

www.clairviewbooks.com

Published by Clairview Books 2019

First published in English by Floris Books, Edinburgh, 2009

Originally published in German under the title *Gespräche mit Bäumen, 1* by
Flensburger Hefte Verlag, Flensburg, 2007

Translated by Matthew Barton
Edited by Wolfgang Weirauch
Illustrated by Gudrun Hofrichter and Jesús Pérez

© Flensburger Hefte 2007
Translation © Floris Books 2009

A CIP catalogue record for this book is available from the British Library

ISBN 978 1 912992 09 6

Cover by Morgan Creative featuring images © Eyetronic & Tomertu
Typeset by Floris Books, Edinburgh
Printed and bound by 4Edge Ltd, Essex

Contents

About the Authors

Verena Staël von Holstein was born in Rendsburg in 1959. She studied surveying and hydrography and worked as a computer programmer and in the hydrographic surveying department. She is a housewife with two children, and lives at a watermill in Lüneburger Heide, a heathland region in Northern Germany. An anthroposophist who sets out to follow Rudolf Steiner's spiritual indications, from childhood onwards she has been able to perceive the etheric and astral realms in human beings and the natural world. She has learnt over many years to train her supersensory perceptions so that communication with nature spirits takes place almost as a matter of course. She receives answers spiritually in the form of patterns, ideas and sometimes also images, and translates them into our human terms. She has been working continuously with nature elementals since she moved to the Mill in 1995.

Wolfgang Weirauch was born in Flensburg in 1953. He studied politics and German literature, then theology at The Christian Community seminary. He publishes the Flensburg Papers series, and teaches politics at Flensburg Waldorf School. He also gives lectures, and teaches on a distance-learning course for Waldorf education and coaching. He received Verena Staël von Holstein's first manuscript Nature Spirits and What They Say in 2001, and soon recognized the value of her conversations with nature elementals. After visiting the Mill and, through Verena, holding meetings where he was able to speak with nature spirits himself, he has published further books of these extraordinary conversations.

Foreword

This is a book of conversations with nature spirits and other spirit beings. There is no general name that applies to all these beings, but they have been called, for instance, elementals, nature spirits or nature beings. The decisive thing is their location, the place of their activity, and the particular task they accomplish.

People often ask us about the best way to come close to nature and the beings enchanted within it. One way to do so is through wonder and astonishment, to open our senses fully to nature's beauty and wisdom. And here we can encounter entities that most closely resemble human beings — the trees. If you give your full attention and interest to trees, approaching them without any kind of egotism, you can learn to love them and, very gradually, perceive the way different trees are related to varying human soul qualities.

As we embarked on this project we wondered, with some trepidation, whether it would prove possible for us to speak with the different tree spirits. But we did. Our efforts were fully rewarded.

Just as nature spirits in previous projects replied to all our questions and spoke to us of supersensible secrets, we were able, through Verena Staël's channelling, to speak with numerous tree spirits and with several tree group souls. The tree spirits replied to all the questions we asked, for instance about the shape of a tree, its role in the landscape, climate change, the relationship of the tree to nature spirits and other domains of the spiritual world, and also about problems specifically affecting trees.

We placed special emphasis on the role of each tree and the human soul quality corresponding to it. The diversity of the human soul is reflected in the distinctive physical form of individual trees.

So we invite you to join us now in these engaging and enthralling conversations, and learn to know and love trees in an entirely new way.

Participating Beings

Theabrox, the Great Timber — wood being
Tutshily, the black cherry — species tree tender
Vux, the sweet cherry — tree being
Ooma, the cherry plum — tree being
Sonar, elder — tree being
Ebsy, the rowan — tree being
Crissie, the European maple — species tree tender
Ella, the black alder — tree being
Kollii, the One from the Marsh — marsh spirit
Petra, the common horse chestnut — tree being
Gunilla, the poplar — species tree tender
Crown, tree tender
Frank, the London plane — tree being
Linda, the lime — species tree tender
Echevit, the Watery One — water being
Lara, the common ash — tree being
Letra, the beech — species tree tender
Robert, the elm — species tree tender
Clausine, the robinia — tree being
Ina, the honey locust — tree being
Birka, the silver or weeping birch — tree being
Cara, the willow — species tree tender
Oakbeen, the oak — tree being
Zuleika, the pomegranate — tree being
Indira, the soapberry — tree being
Gunda, the boswellia or frankincense — tree being
Miller, the House Spirit
Paolo, palo santo — tree being
Olivia, the olive — tree being

Elemental Beings

Gnomes — elementals of the earth
Undines — elementals of water
Sylphs — elementals of the air
Salamanders — elementals of fire

Theabrox, the Great Timber

Theabrox: Hello, I like the thought of a tree book, and we are pleased to help.

WW: Hello Theabrox. In your view, what is a tree?

Theabrox: A tree is a special type of being. It is an image of the human being, reflected onto the plant realm. That's the most important thing we experience, initially, with trees. Most people have a certain idea about nymphs, but nymphs are not the same as tree spirits. Tree nymphs live in trees, of course, but they are not tree spirits. They have a close connection with the tree; but if you talk to Oakbeen, for example, this is not a nymph but the self of one of the oaks standing here in front of the house.

WW: And what are nymphs?

Theabrox: Nymphs (tree tenders) are beings closely connected with the tree-self. Somehow they have a feminine character. They look after the tree and care for it, but they are not the tree-self. It is similar to the relationship between you and the elemental being or spirit of your body: you are the self or the I; the elemental spirit of your body dwells in you but is not your self. All trees we have talked to so far are either the respective selves of the trees, or the greater, overarching tree beings. For example, Cordon is not the body elemental of an individual person, but a higher elemental of a particular region. In just the same way there are spirit tree tenders for a certain region, though these are not necessarily the higher ones such as Crown.

The tree in material terms

Like human beings, a tree has various bodies; but the difference is that these are not all present in earthly existence. Some of these tree bodies — and this is hard to express or understand — are situated in parallel earths or worlds, that is, in certain realms of the world of spirit. You call these realms Lower or Higher Devachan but these expressions don't really come from your own central European culture. When you are embodied, incarnated as human beings, your bodies — from the physical body through to the I — are more or less embodied together; this is not the case with a tree, for while its physical body stands here or there in a wood, its I dwells in the world of spirit.

In physical terms the tree also has various parts, such as the root, the trunk and branches, and the crown with its leaves — to mention just three typical aspects of the tree. If a plant does not have this threefold division, you can't really call it a tree. If the crown grows directly from the ground you call it a bush, for it doesn't have a trunk like a tree does. Of course, there are always intermediate types. The tree's roots usually delve into the ground, but sometimes into water as well. And then there are fascinating trees like the mangroves that grow partly in the water, partly above it, and only connect minimally with the soil. They have a trunk and are quite open above and below.

Generally roots penetrate the earth and sometimes even stone, for a tree has enormous strength in its roots. Every homeowner who has a tree standing too close to his house knows of this problem.

The root region of the tree corresponds to the head in humans. If you people were trees, one would first have to lodge you head-down in the soil. Then comes the trunk, subdivided into bark, phloem, cambium, xylem and core. The first protects the tree, the next transports sugars between roots and leaves: the cambium is the layer of cells which multiply, and in the xylem, minerals and water are carried up from the roots. Then you have the crown with twigs and leaves; and here you find all kinds of shapes, varying greatly from one type of tree to another.

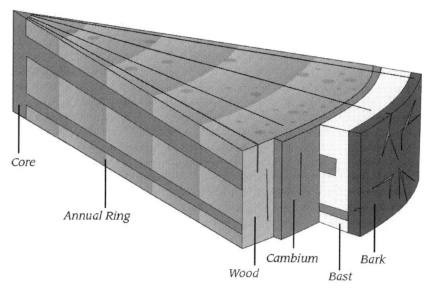

Core

Annual Ring

Cambium   Bark

Wood   Bast

Cross-section through a five-year-old pine trunk

Each crown will have evergreen or deciduous leaves. The leaves themselves have very varied forms — from palm leaves through to birch leaves, from heart-shaped to pinnate, from smooth-edged to serrated, from thick and fleshy through to fine and delicate leaves. Most leaves are green, though some are red or other colours. The leaves are the area of the tree where it enters into contact with the air and atmosphere. What trees exhale through their leaves is what people like to breathe in — that is, oxygen. If trees no longer existed, the lungs of the oceans would still breathe, it is true, but things would be very difficult for the world and human beings.

Human being and tree

WW: You compare trees with people. Where do the parallels really lie here, for instance between the human head and the tree roots?

Theabrox: That's self-evident. Through its roots the tree engages with the contracted and enclosed mineral world, and absorbs the world's mineral constituents. Naturally it also absorbs cosmic forces that are connected with these constituents. This corresponds with the area in you in which your physical body enters into a closed form and where minerals are most strongly represented: the domain of the human head. The leafy part of a tree corresponds with human breathing, and the trunk with its branches to the will realm, the human being's limb system.

Tree spirits, tenders and other elemental beings

WW: What is a tree spirit exactly? What tasks does it perform and, in doing so, what relationship does it have with other elemental beings?

Theabrox: The tree spirit is the self of the tree but does not have its I within it as people do. It only has limited access to the I of the tree, which is located in the world of spirit. The tree spirit is closely linked with its body elemental, and in fact it *is* this spirit really. Then there is also the tree tender, that is, the nymph. There can be several of these to each tree. The nymph can separate itself from the tree whereas the tree spirit cannot do so.

WW: When and why do nymphs separate themselves from trees?

Theabrox: They also work in the tree's surroundings and can be elsewhere too, in spatial terms. When I say 'separate' I don't mean that they go away forever, but that they can remove themselves etherically and spatially from the tree because they are active elsewhere. Then they return again. A tree spirit on the other hand must always be connected with a tree. Nymphs do not separate entirely from a tree, for then they would suffer very badly. They work in the tree's surroundings, usually not very far away.

WW: What relationship does a tree have — or rather the beings within it — to other elemental beings?

Theabrox: They have very close relationships with a great many elementals—with the gnomes, undines, sylphs and salamanders. Their relationship to the salamanders is not the most intense but does occur in connection with fruit formation. The gnomes work in the root realm, helping to conduct minerals there. There is a great circulation of water in the tree, in which the undines are involved. The undines are very diverse in nature.

There are miniscule ones right through to beings the size of Echevit. Echevit is a different and higher being but he too has something of an undine quality. Sylphs on the other hand live and work in the tree crowns, and sometimes they congregate there. This is especially the case when the trees bear blossom. Trees find difficulty only with the direct and manifest form of the salamanders. They naturally collaborate in the weaving of warmth, in fruit formation.

Contacting tree beings

Wolfgang Weirauch: I have sought out a few dozen trees and
  formulated some questions for them, which I will now ask in
  sequence. You must then see which of you would like to reply.
Theabrox: First I have a question for you. Would you like to speak
  directly with the trees themselves, or do you wish to speak to
  me about them?
WW: I'm surprised that it's possible for me to speak with individual
  trees, but if so let's do it that way. You can always add anything
  you think is necessary. Decide amongst yourselves what will
  work best.
Theabrox: By saying this you allow us scope for freedom. It
  is possible for Verena to make contact with the individual
  trees through me and the tree tenders. The leaves you have
  collected come from trees which all grow several hundred
  kilometres from here. However, we can make contact with
  each respective tree being. So we can call on each tree, such
  as Oakbeen, or the oak, which stands right here in front of
  the house, and which you can touch. We can also invoke the
  mothers of all tree species: this is an intermediate level which
  we didn't have until now. Instead of Oakbeen, the single oak,
  we could therefore equally speak with the Great Oak. Over
  and above this there are also the tree-tending beings — for
  instance myself as timber being, and the tree tenders, which
  have less to do with the wood itself, and more to do with how
  individual trees may spread or withdraw. We can contact all
  these beings; we can also just see how things develop.
WW: That would be best of all. The order in which we speak to
  them doesn't matter. I simply collected leaves, pressed them
  and placed them in a box. Let's start with the topmost leaf. The
  first tree is a wild cherry.
Theabrox: That's fitting, for you are a cherry-tree person, though
  not a wild cherry person. So I'm not surprised that you chose
  cherry to begin with.

The Black Cherry

Prunus serotina

Theabrox: This is a cherry tree which grows close to the edge of a wood.

WW: That's right.

Verena Staël von Holstein: I'm always amazed when these things prove correct.

Theabrox: This wild cherry is widespread with you and is a tree typical of the region.

WW: What can you tell me about it?

Theabrox: Are you clear which this is? There are two main types of wild cherry, the European and the American late-flowering black cherry. The American black cherry found its way here a few hundred years ago and has spread far and wide. For us it is a problematic tree being; it is an imported tree that in many places has more or less driven away the indigenous kind. The leaf you brought with you is not the European but the American kind.

WW: Why do these late-flowering black cherry trees grow so abundantly in hedgerows and parks?

Theabrox: Because they have no European competitors. This is the big problem with plants that come from other countries: they have no corresponding pests. Tree nature is only in equilibrium if the trees have adversaries. Only then can balance arise.

The tree has not yet shaken off its American past

WW: Do you mean tree adversaries, or other creatures?

Theabrox: Both — adversaries in the form of competitor trees, insects, birds and other animals. The late-flowering black cherry does not have adversaries because the spirits of creation did not plan it for the European context. It was dragged in here — something very easy actually, for you only need a cherry stone.

But this wild cherry blossoms very beautifully, and around the end of May it looks magical. When flowering it also has a very pleasant scent. Its blossoms are white. This tree has not yet shaken off its American past. In your way of marking time it will take a few hundred years before it becomes European. That is why it still has a strongly proliferative and unconstrained quality. There are so many of these wild cherry trees! They provide the birds with a good basis for their diet,

and spread very abundantly through bird excrement. This wild cherry grows very fast and thus easily suppresses indigenous species. Most people like this tree very much because of its pleasant appearance.

Originally this cherry was exported to bring a touch of beauty to European parks. But then it spread rapidly across great swathes of northern Europe — and now here comes the American black cherry's overarching being.

Only few can speak to me

WW: Hello.

Tutshily: Hello.

WW: What kind of being are you?

Tutshily: I am the European aspect of the American black cherry, the late-flowering black cherry. I tend the various cherry tree beings, concerning myself with the overall stocks of cherries and sometimes also with individual cherry trees. If I can express this in human terms, I lead the negotiations of my species with the European trees, and try to reach consensus with them.

You people brought me over here to Europe and left me to my own devices. This happened a few hundred years ago and now you are trying to regulate my triumphant spread through Europe. As higher tree being I try to bring this situation into balance. However, this is relatively difficult, as only a few people can speak to me.

The shape of the leaves reveals our character

WW: I would be glad to hear something about the shape of the leaves. Why are they so long and oval, and why do they end in such a sharp point?

Tutshily: The shape of the leaves has a great deal to do with our interaction with sylphs, for the leaves are the organs we breathe with — if we may compare this with you humans. The sun shines on the leaves and the sunlight helps give us the energy to form sugars we need to grow. At the same time this enables us to form chlorophyll and to organize our breathing processes.

The shape of the leaves reveals our character. The shape of the black cherry leaves has something primitive and knife-like. If you observe ancient stone knives, they have a very similar form. This also highlights our capacity to defend ourselves and conquer terrains.

Secondly the narrowness of the leaves shows that we are very good at surviving droughts. The narrower a leaf, the less water evaporates from its surface. We have many narrow leaves. We are able to relinquish some leaves while continuing to work with the others. The shape of the leaf shows also whether trees — in this case we black cherries — can cope well with dryness. We can.

The slight serration on the leaf edge shows that we have a certain aggression. Such serration always has something to do with the capacity to assert yourself.

WW: On the leaf stalk there are meant to be two red glands, though you can't see them on this leaf. What are they for?

Tutshily: Sap can be exuded there, and nectar is secreted which certain creatures can ingest. But for some creatures this nectar is poisonous. That's why we are relatively good at defending ourselves against pests.

We are also very fast growing. If you break us, we quickly put out new growth from the broken place.

The strong scent expresses our conquering character

WW: Why do your blossoms have such a strong scent and such a beautiful shape?

Tutshily: Our blossom is almost pure white and the pollen is strongly dispersed. We're not an ideal tree for people with allergies. If as a tree you emit a strong scent, it attracts many insects, and so many fruits form and, in turn, many new trees grow. We are certainly not reticent in character.

We cope with various different soils, moist as well as dry, sandy soils. We grow both in hedgerows and in damper meadow areas. However we can't tolerate severe cold, which is why we don't spread into far northern and high mountainous regions. Our nature is both to be fast growing and to have beautiful flowers, which gives us a seductive character. People like growing us and overlook the fact that we can suppress other plants.

The Native Americans made nectar and medicines from our glands, and these played an important role in North American culture. However, knowledge of these medicines vanished with the demise of these people.

Help for the skin

WW: What medicine did the Indians make from you?

Tutshily: They made a skin cream that helped wounds heal and form good scar tissue. Based on this, research could be done today to give you some benefit from my tree expertise.

WW: Would this medicine help us today?

Tutshily: Yes, for eczema, and for all rupturing skin diseases. We heal the skin and help it to close up again. The fact that we are very strong growers means we quickly seal up our boundaries.

My berries are bitter

WW: Why are your berries so small and bitter?

Tutshily: We aren't poisonous for people, though our berries don't taste good to you. And our berries are small so that smaller animals can manage them. Our berries are eaten in great numbers by your European songbirds because they are the right size for them to eat easily. That's very advantageous for us: the birds provide us with a good means of spreading. The berries are sour or bitter because they contain tannin, but this doesn't deter the animals.

WW: In late summer we see starlings sitting on high-voltage power lines, and below, the ground is covered in cherry stones. Do they spit out the stones, or do these pass through their digestion?

Tutshily: Normally the whole cherry is swallowed and the stones are excreted. Most creatures, particularly birds, have very strong stomach acids because they often cannot chew. That is why you find scarcely any excrement near the cherry stones, and the stones themselves look chewed up.

WW: Why are the berries first yellow, then red, and finally black?

Tutshily: That's part of our seduction principle: it's very attractive to first see yellow, then red, then black berries. Yellow is a warning colour that tells creatures the berries aren't yet ripe. Many poison-bearing animals also have yellow markings, such as wasps or various snakes. Red is also a warning colour, though not such a definite one. Black is a sign to the birds that the cherries are now sweet.

WW: Why do wild cherries have such a large stone relative to the fruit?

Tutshily: Because we are Americans. Much that grows on the American continent gets very big compared with European conditions. We don't have the highest mountains there, but we do have the deepest canyon, and people there also tend to keep getting bigger. I cannot tell you why America has the task of making things big — you'd have to ask higher beings.

Be seductive!

WW: What is the difference between you wild cherries and the so-called sweet cherry?

Tutshily: Sweet cherries got big because people intentionally bred them. The normal European wild cherry also has smaller fruits, similar to the American type. People bred the sweet cherry from the European wild cherry, cultivating it for sweetness and richer fruit flesh. The sweet cherry also has a very strong seductive impetus. If a cherry tree grows by a fence, hardly anyone can pass without picking a cherry. One of our life principles, endowed by the spirits of creation, is: be seductive! The seductive tree!

WW: If we were to look for a parallel between the cherry tree and a human soul quality, would that be seduction and persuasiveness?

Tutshily: Yes. If you transpose our qualities to people, you get a relatively innocent power of seduction. Nothing like vampirism. The cherry tree corresponds to a relatively innocent, yet still somewhat sexually seductive principle. Sweet cherries are also often compared with girls' lips. This is really a youthful seductiveness. All cherries have something delicate, and likewise our leaves are not large and fleshy.

Sweet and sour

WW: The wild cherries include dark-sapped ones from which the sweet cherries derive, and light-sapped varieties. What is the difference between these two kinds?

Tutshily: The dark colour gives more sugariness. When you melt sugar in a pan it goes brown. Every sugar is first brown and is only bleached later. If you want to know why sweetness has a brown colour, you'll again have to ask another being.

WW: There is also a third kind of cherry, the sour cherries. What kind are they?

Tutshily: The sour cherry is the one you can store: that's due to the acidity it contains. You can't really store or freeze sweet cherries, as usually they'll just turn to pulp. This is because sweet cherries don't retain formative powers. Acidity — corresponding to pain in humans — gives form. That's why sour cherries are the ones which you humans can store. People also put sour cherries on cakes and use sweet cherries for sauces.

WW: What can you say about cherry wood?

Tutshily: I myself am more bush-like. Cherry wood from true sweet cherry trees has a different quality. This is a very beautiful and hard wood; it has a fine grain and is suitable for making furniture and musical instruments. Furniture made of cherry wood used to be for the 'best drawing room.' People used not to like felling cherry trees, until they grew old and no longer bore so well.

Pushing other cultures away

WW: What relationship do you cherry trees have to people?

Tutshily: We need humans because they spread us. We have the tendency to spread far and wide — a quality that also comes from the continent where we originate. To ensure this, people have to be tempted by us to carry us across the globe. We belong to the American way of life and represent this somewhat as trees: seductive, proliferative, pretty to look at, but also pushing other cultures away. It's hard to keep us within bounds. We aren't a tree for jungles far from human habitation, unless people carry us there. We follow civilization. We can't grow next to great trees that deprive us of light. We need marginal areas, hedges or park-like landscapes. You have many such areas, particularly in Schleswig-Holstein.

WW: What can you tell me about the stripes on the bark of the sweet cherry?

Verena Staël von Holstein: Now Vux, the sweet cherry, is coming. Tutshily no longer feels able to reply to this.

The Sweet Cherry

Prunus avium

Vux: I am a tree that has been bred by humans. I didn't exist originally, though I've been around for a relatively long time now.
The sweet cherry is one of the early-blossoming trees, flowering before its leaves appear. The stripes of our bark and the
fact that the bark peels off in strips attract insects which are
needed for fertilizing our blossoms. The striation on our bark
draws fertilizing insects. Every tree has its own way of regu-
lating these processes. For instance, the oak needs no bees to
fertilize it, and has a quite different, rather repelling bark.

WW: Sap often oozes from cherry trees.

Vux: This sap attracts the insects and also has a somewhat
seductive quality. It's not just the American cherries that have
this, but also the European cherries.

It is interesting that our cherries grow in a quite different
shape, for the sweet cherry does not have such large clusters.
If the cherries grew in large bunches, they would obstruct each
other.

WW: Does the sap from the trunk of the cherry tree also help heal any human illnesses?

Vux: This sap has not yet been used in the proper way. It would prevent skin ulceration processes. Many medicines could be obtained from trees. The sap from the cherry tree also helps against coughs and worms.

The cherry-eating path of self-development

WW: What happens in us when we eat a cherry?

Vux: You have a pronounced sensory experience as you become aware of the cherry's smoothness. Pleasant sensations come both from the tactile experience of the cherry on the tongue and also the taste of the sweet cherry juice. The consistency of the cherry flesh as you chew is also pleasant. But then comes the shock of the fact that the cherry contains something hard. This shows you have to be careful while chewing; and that something hard surfaces behind the youthful and seductive quality. After youthful seduction something else must arise, for otherwise life would not continue. So biting and chewing a cherry can be a kind of schooling: if you reflect on the cherry fruit you will realize that a stony principle holds sway behind the plump, bright, seductive cherry fruit.

WW: What occurs in soul terms in the mouth and in the whole human being when we eat a sour cherry?

Vux: When you eat a sour cherry you have both things at once: it's not just sour but sweet too. In fact this corresponds to the human being in the period after puberty, when he realizes that life isn't just terrible or beautiful but that he also possesses inner forces and is capable of devotion — that life is not only sweet but that humans also grow riper. The stone of the sweet cherry is equally hard however. But underlying this is something spiritual. In the stone a very high spiritual principle is indicated in fact. The harder something is, the higher the spiritual principle.

The freshness of youth could vanish from the world

WW: Is there anything else to say about cherry trees in general that we haven't mentioned yet?

Vux: Cherry trees have a problem. Due to the massive changes in our environment and climate, we are unable to ripen sufficiently, as it's too wet in spring, and too dry afterwards. So we cannot form fruits properly any more; we can no longer fully display our seductive arts. We come into fluid movement too soon, and then there is no fluid left when we really need it because the weather is too dry. We can't form cherries so well now, and the creatures don't enjoy eating us so much; and this means we don't spread so easily. The huge shift in growth cycles that has arisen due to climate change leads to diminishing sweet seduction and youthfulness in the world. Or it will only appear in the rampant growth of the late-flowering black cherry, which is much less susceptible to climate change. But if you don't watch out, the culture of youthful growth will vanish.

The Cherry Plum

Prunus cerasifera

WW: What is the nature of this ornamental tree?

Ooma: We don't come from Europe but from Asia

WW: And who are you?

Ooma: A cherry plum. We are Asiatic ornamental trees. The Asiatic peoples have a very special relationship with the cherry as they themselves are ancient in type. That's why they have a particular desire to see something fresh and youthful. This is rather like old people taking pleasure in watching young children, because the difference and distance between them is so great. The relationship between Asiatic peoples and the cherries is similar. You can see this especially with the Japanese and their Japanese cherries, for instance in their cherry blossom festivals.

I myself am a cross between a plum and a cherry. I was conceived as an ornamental tree, not to give edible fruit. I belong to the culture of stylized Chinese-Japanese gardens The colour of the leaves is an important aspect of my tree. In Asia the plum is traditionally a tree from which alcoholic drinks are derived. The youthfulness of the cherry has been combined with the plum. My type of tree arose from human cultivation.

I grow relatively slowly and I grow tall, and people like planting me in parks and front gardens. Since I grow slowly I am easier to manage. I try to combine the principle of youth with that of early old age, of sedate maturity.

The Black Elder

Sambucus nigra

WW: What human qualities resemble the elder being?
Sonar: The human quality that resembles me is femininity, but of
a kind not yet governed by the I.

Gateway to the world of spirit

For human beings there are various paths to seek initiation into
the world of spirit: firstly through thinking, clarity of thought;
then the path which corresponds more to me is a path rooted
in one's own culture. The latter requires a place individually
suited to it, to perceive a transition into spiritual realities. On

the one hand such a person needs to
be formed in a relatively gnarled way,
but on the other hand he needs an
unimpeded lightness — as you find in
my timber. From the outside my wood
looks completely gnarled, but inside I
am almost cotton-like. As trees, we need

a harder exterior form, but within I'm the opposite of heaviness: a matter that is almost dissolving. This shows that I'm a kind of connecting radiance between this world and the world of spirit. This primarily corresponded with people in ancient times, but it is still so for people who have the right capacity. The people of former times, who were still in a more reflective state, were at home beside me, between the worlds. This permeation with spirit informs my whole being and substance.

Leaves which cut their way into the world of spirit

On the one hand my substance is very stable, on the other it is in dissolution. For instance, see the feathery quality of my pinnate leaves, through to the tips of each leaf, which are pointed and dentate, or toothed. Due to my transitional and gateway function, my leaves are flame shaped. In the flame you meet the world of spirit in tangible form.

WW: And where does the sharp serration of individual leaves come from?

Sonar: That is the flame form.

WW: I can see the flame form in a whole individual leaf, but flames don't have marginal teeth.

Sonar: The dentate shape shows, on the one hand, the power of dissolution, and on the other that one needs a certain strength of persistence to enter the world of spirit; this too is expressed in the teeth of my leaves. In a certain way one has to cut one's way into the world of spirit. Every jag has an opening, but is also saw-like in character.

Luciferic and Ahrimanic

WW: When your leaves are rubbed they give off an unpleasant smell, for us at least. Why is this?

Sonar: A sulphurous quality comes

through here. The world of spirit does not necessarily smell very good for earthly senses. You would need to completely refashion your sense systems to really endure spirituality. If you want to develop your clairsentient faculties of smell, you can school your senses with the scent of crumbled elder leaf. On the other hand, my blossoms give off a fragrance that you probably find wonderful, which has an intoxicating effect and which you can also use to make sparkling wine. The scent serves at the same time as a warning not to get intoxicated.

WW: I don't quite understand what you mean by a warning against intoxication.

Sonar: We European plants always have something of the quality of a finger raised in warning. The sulphurous aroma is also a kind of warning; and you know of course who the lord of sulphur is!

WW: Are you referring to Ahriman?

Sonar: Yes. In our blossoms we have a luciferic quality, and in our leaves something ahrimanic. Both aspects are important for properly grasping the world of spirit. As human you cannot properly perceive the world of spirit without an awareness of both Lucifer and Ahriman. If I serve, as plant, as passageway to the world of spirit, I must have aspects of both within me.

The guardian of the threshold

WW: Are the fruits the balance between these?

Sonar: My fruits have a strong healing effect. The ripe berries are an anti-fever medicine and in a certain sense dispel the intoxicated state of fever. The healing spirit also lives in me in a recuperative capacity. In former times people fortified themselves with elderberry juice against winter illnesses.

WW: Why are the unripe, green fruits harmful to health, especially for children?

Sonar: When you are still green you should not pass across to the other side, for then spirituality can endanger you. You first have to attain a certain soul maturity to cope with the full reality. The guardian of the threshold and I have a very close relationship. Wherever elder grows you can encounter your guardian. Wherever I grow the guardians of the threshold feel good. For you humans it is probably very confusing when I speak of guardians in the plural. Really there is only one, but each person has a very strong individual participation in this guardian. The moment a person encounters the guardian of the threshold, the latter becomes his personal guardian of the threshold. The guardian reflects you. He holds up a mirror that shows you everything within you of which you are unaware. The encounter with the guardian of the threshold is an extraordinarily intimate experience. Every person has his own threshold, of course, and must find his own way into the spiritual world. You cannot cross over by Verena's threshold, and she cannot cross by yours.

WW: What is the nature of this encounter with the guardian of the threshold today? Rudolf Steiner writes that it is now high time to meet the guardian, at least once in one's life. On the other hand, it is certain that next to no one does so, among other things because of the strong distractions of life today. Can you comment on this problem?

Sonar: There's a great deal to say about this. In fact many people do encounter their guardian, but are not aware of it. This often happens through illnesses, also psychotic ones. But people do not penetrate this experience with their clear consciousness. People need a certain schooling to consciously perceive and penetrate a guardian experience. All threshold experiences are really guardian experiences, even if you do not perceive them as such. In near-death experiences too, people encounter their guardian, even if they are unaware of it. Some even meet the great guardian, Christ. He is the figure of light who stands there.

It is therefore true to say that most people do not manage to consciously invoke an experience of the guardian. On the other hand these guardian experiences are silently interwoven with each person's biography, in illnesses, crises or other catastrophes.

As a tree I find it very important that you have such conscious experiences of awakening. In the outer world the climate is slipping beyond your control, your own biographies are slipping out of your grasp in the personal realm, and illnesses are getting beyond your control too: all these things are the result of you failing to work with the world of spirit. That many people no longer want to die and want to delay death, the pursuit of youthfulness, and that cancer is so widespread — these are signs that you are growing distant from the world of spirit. I am *not* saying that someone with cancer cannot experience the guardian. All these are just general tendencies.

Be masters of your time

WW: What would humans need to change in order to have a conscious guardian experience?

Sonar: You should take more time for important things. You can start with very small steps and for instance simply take time to play with a child. That will make your life less hectic. Most people simply no longer have the time to sit down and consciously invoke an experience of the guardian. You should become masters of your time. Organize your time so that this is possible.

WW: What healing effects do your bark, berries and leaves have?

Sonar: Our bark contains salicylic acid, which people have used in aspirin, though there are other trees that contain more of it. Elder also counteracts worms and heals intestinal illnesses. The main use for elderberries is as warming remedy for colds and chills and to help bring out a strong fever. If you have asthma and breathe for a while through a hollowed-out elder twig, you will breathe more easily. People have forgotten about this. Elder has a cleansing effect on the body. You can't cross over the threshold in an impure state.

WW: Where do these protective and cleansing forces of elder come from? Who gave them to you?

Sonar: The spirits of creation. They agreed it amongst themselves. I belong to the cultural inheritance of northern Europe, and thus to the forces that come from the North and Teutonic cultures. I belong to people of the central European cultural epoch and their roots. In planning these cultural epochs, the spirits of creation configured me as a tree. I am not so important for Asiatic peoples.

WW: There are said to have been times when people took off their hats as a mark of respect when passing an elder tree. Why did they do this?

Sonar: Because they knew unconsciously that the place surrounding an elder tree is sacred. That's why they removed their hats in the same way as going into church. At the same time people knew unconsciously that higher beings were connected with the elder tree, such as the guardian of the threshold, or Mother Holle, who is a fairytale image of the figure of the guardian.

WW: Is there anything more you would like to say?

Sonar: We could fill a whole book together, about the encounter with the spiritual world and illnesses that can be cured with me. But that would take us too far now.

WW: Many thanks.

Sonar: My pleasure. I always enjoy speaking to you.

The Rowan Tree

Sorbus aucuparia

WW: The mountain ash or rowan has pinnate leaves, each with nine to nineteen leaflets — many more therefore than the elder leaf. What is the difference between your leaf and the elder's?

Ebsy: Good day. I am very resilient; you can't get rid of me. Rowans grow almost everywhere. You can also eat rowan berries. People used to make jam or jelly with me, but that's gone out of fashion. I don't know why.

The sylphs play through my leaves

WW: Is there spiritual significance in the fact that your compound leaves have smaller leaflets?

Ebsy: Everything has spiritual significance. My pinnate leaves are quite different from those of the elder. My leaf is relatively long and narrow, whereas the elder leaf is much broader. I don't have a tongue or flame shape

in my leaf, nor much relationship with the flame. However, due to my pinnate nature I do symbolize a certain openness to the world of spirit; at the same time this feathery quality also points to the element of air. The sylphs are very fond of me because they can play through my leaves.

I am a practical tree

At the same time, in contrast to the elder, I am not at all knotty or gnarled but my wood is extremely elastic. I can grow where almost nothing else can, for instance on rubbish dumps. This enables me to bring a light-filled spirituality back to places which are devoid of it. My roots penetrate the earth around me with forces of light and air. I root where other types of trees cannot. I am found in great numbers and am not really endangered.

The only tree or bush that causes me concern is the late-flowering black cherry — the American variety — for it grows in my indigenous locations. The rowan's practical light-pervading stance has to make way for the black cherry's seductive principle, something one could almost regard as symptomatic of our current times. I am really a very practical tree, and my berries have many uses. This is not true of the berries of the late-flowering black cherry. My wood can be used to make many things, whereas no one has yet made anything useful with black cherry wood.

WW: It seems, therefore, that you compete with each other because you grow in the same places?

Ebsy: That's right.

A spear-point of Michael

WW: In the autumn your foliage turns yellow through to red, like the leaves of various other trees. Where does this yellow and red colouring come from?

Ebsy: I am a child of the light and air, and these elements are assigned to Michael as lord of our epoch. Michael belongs to the autumn, and that is why I assume the colours of light in autumn. I temporarily become golden like the sunlight. And when people look at me they think of light. In this way Michael can become more conscious in them. In my leaves, therefore, a Michael presence approaches human beings.

WW: How do you explain the red?

Ebsy: Red reveals Michael's combative aspect. He is both light-filled on the one hand and combative and repelling on the other. This gesture of warding off is directed towards the ahrimanic world in particular. My berries acquire a red colour when the season is turning colder, and ahrimanic power is gaining strength towards winter. My red reveals that, with Michael, I combatively oppose this tendency of the season. This red coloration can be seen both in my leaves and also in my berries. My berries are very nutritious and sustain fresh and vital forces in those who eat them. This is also important for meeting Ahriman with strength.

WW: Why do some of these berries stay hanging on the trees in winter?

Ebsy: In winter the berries serve as food for the birds. There's a hunter's saying about me in Germany: 'When the rowan's red as coral, then the red deer's full-grown and must fall.'

WW: Your blossoms are white, umbel-like clusters. What does this express?

Ebsy: The panicle is small and fine-blossomed. This fine structure expresses my dedication to the airy, light-filled element. Its narrow, lancet-like shape also reveals a kind of spear-point of Michael, for Michael holds this spear-point or sword-point against the dragon. I am absolutely a Michael tree.

WW: What is expressed in the shining, smooth grey bark of the rowan trunk?

Ebsy: It is a good shield against all outer influences. The smooth trunk or bark of the rowan means it is hard to wound. All that is dark, evil or cold slides off it. But I am not a typical medicinal plant: I am not nearly so mystical.

I will cope

WW: What human qualities correspond to you?

Ebsy: A sanguine disposition in people points most in my direction. I'm thinking here of very active people with a range of different gestures, who like dressing in cheerful, colourful clothes. The human type of the positive autumn person best corresponds to me. My nature most closely relates to people who get on with things and make the most of modest circumstances, who say yes to life and who aren't easily ground down.

WW: The rowan looks particularly beautiful in autumn when it bears red umbels. What effect does this tree have on people?

Ebsy: Michael! Light and beauty! People often don't really look at us and dismiss us, but this beauty is in us. If someone looks at me in autumn, he absorbs a Michaelic quality. He turns towards the element of light, on the one hand with a somewhat combative aspect, expressed in the red berries, and on the other with the light-imbued element that spreads through the world as streams of thought. You spread light through your soul when you absorb my image. When you meditate on me you are brighter afterwards. I embody thought-borne action.

WW: Your character is somehow that of a very practical tree.

Ebsy: I am very practical. If I were human I would be a very practical person, though not the most reflective. I can absorb many thoughts but I don't dwell on things. I care very well for the soil on which I grow. I also get on well with the stinging nettle. The only being that troubles me is the late-flowering black cherry.

WW: Why is it that you are so undemanding about soils, growing both in lowlands and in mountainous regions, and that even in cold years you grow relatively well?

Ebsy: Because I get whatever I need. I scarcely need the soil for I give back more than I take from it; I improve it through my qualities of light. Michael, you can say, is similarly undemanding.

WW: Can you explain that?

Ebsy: I mean it quite simply. He does nothing for himself. He is selfless. You could also look at it the other way round. Michael has the high task of embodying the countenance of Christ, to stand as shield before Christ. This is a great demand upon him, but he himself stands before Christ without demands of his own.

WW: You are the most northerly-growing hardwood. Why?

Ebsy: The birch also comes very far north. I survive well in the cold for my Michaelic powers are good at resisting Ahriman. In the far north, particularly, you have a great deal of darkness on the one hand — but I'm well armed against this — and yet on the other a great deal of light. This supports my nature. It is only hard for me to grow under tall firs, although I do grow in clearings. I don't grow in the thick forest, nor under tall beeches. I am more suited to the edge of the wood.

WW: What can you say about your timber?

Ebsy: It is highly elastic and pliable. I can be used for plaiting and basket weaving although willow is better. Despite this elasticity, I am very hard, and people of former times used to use me, among other things, for cudgel fighting. Ordinary people didn't have metal weapons, so they used rowan wood.

WW: More recently people have found that the quality of rowan wood is good for things like furniture.

Ebsy: Yes, I'm also good for making wooden pegs and screws, since my wood is highly resilient. The problem is that I don't form trunks as thick as other trees, and people therefore don't plant me as a timber crop. I look lovely but I'm not wide in girth.

WW: We already mentioned that in autumn and at the onset of winter you provide birds with an alternative when there are no insects.

Ebsy: Not just for birds but also squirrels and many other small creatures. When our berries fall they provide mice with winter stores as well. We are a plant that is particularly beneficial in autumn. If there were no rowans in northern Germany this would be a catastrophe for many creatures.

Defence against the dragon

WW: The rowan tree also has mythological significance and was dedicated to the Teutonic god Donar. The druids made their magic staffs from rowan wood, and these trees were planted around oracle and judgment sites. Why?

Ebsy: Donar is a difficult god, and there's a confusion relating to him. Some people equate Donar with Thor, others with Wotan or Odin. I belong to Odin. Odin occupies a place amongst the Michaelic hosts, and he and his son Vidar collaborate very closely with Michael. Nowadays — if you still experience anything — you experience the angels as gods. In the Greek and Roman era people built temples to the archangels. In the preceding cultural epoch people's experience of the divine focused on the archai. The Persians experienced the exusiai as their gods, the ancient Indians invoked the dynamis. Michael has a particular relationship with every cultural epoch, and thus also with Odin, the Teutonic god, chief of the Aesir. Odin is really also an archangel and he and his son Vidar are really Michaelic gods. This is why people who used to live under the sway of these gods made their magic staffs from my wood.

WW: People even used to believe that rowan twigs would protect them against dragons, and they hung them on the walls of their houses and in their byres. Is this also connected with the fact that you are a Michaelic tree?

Ebsy: Of course.

WW: How real is this? If one actually hangs a rowan twig in one's house or barn, does this offer real protection against small dragons?

Ebsy: Such twigs primarily help defend you against ahrimanic dragons, but not luciferic ones. You can also hang rowan wood above your front door, which will give you a very practical defence against any ahrimanic impulse that seeks to gain entry. Wood like that does offer a certain resistance.

WW: But how exactly? People themselves are the greatest dragons and they bring small ahrimanic demons with them into a house.

Ebsy: When someone imbued with an ahrimanic quality walks under rowan wood, his ahrimanic forces are weakened. If someone allies himself more or less with Ahriman, he takes the latter's outlook with him everywhere, of course. But such a person can find his power enhanced or diminished. If someone is unconsciously connected with Ahriman, for instance the postman, and he comes close to this rowan twig, it will actually help him. In the rowan invisible forces are active. The elemental world is enormously diverse.

WW: Can one also place the twig in a room?

Ebsy: Of course — but not under a pile of newspapers. It needs to be visible: if you conceal me I cannot work so well. For instance, it would be good to hang me from the ceiling.

WW: Is there anything else you would like to say?

Ebsy: Take more notice of the rowan! Allow my Michaelic forces to help you. When making autumn decorations, include the rowan. I would be glad.

WW: What healing effects do the rowan's leaves and blossoms have?

Ebsy: I chiefly have a vitalizing and protecting effect, but I cannot compare myself with the elder. Michael is not the great healer; that is not his task. If you cut yourself you can bind one of my leaves over the wound. It will help, but there are more medicinal plants.

Maple

The Norway Maple

Acer platanoides

WW: The leaves of the Norway maple have five lobes with three main lobes, each ending in several points. There is a striking contrast in the round concavities between the jagged points. What does this leaf shape express?

Theabrox: First of all we can compare this with another phenomenon in nature — the water drop. In its leaf the maple shows that substance is dripping out. There are a great many varieties of maple, for instance the European and North American. In Canada they even have the maple leaf on their flag. The Norway maple is not a European variety but typically North American, in which the maple shape and the drop-like quality are most clearly expressed. All kinds of maple also have five lobes. Five is the number of Jupiter.

WW: Why? Is this based on the various embodiments of the earth that Steiner refers to?

Theabrox: No, not that, but the number five is generally assigned to Jupiter. Four is the number of the earth, five of Jupiter — and at the same time the number representative of the human being. This can also be seen in the pentacle or pentagram. People regard the pentagram in many different ways: some find it fore-

boding whereas others see it as a herald of the future. In four you find the opened cross. The fifth level is the future human being who has come into possession of the fifth aspect of his being — but then, in the Jupiter state, the physical body falls away and a fourfold division remains. The human I or ego is embodied in fourfold structure.

Light substance trickles out

The Norway maple therefore contains the shape of a water drop, or rather stalactite. The maple is a plant that colours strongly in autumn. You could say that light substance trickles out from it. Accordingly, we find a principle similar to that we just saw with the rowan, although the maple leaf is not in the least pinnate; the incisions in the maple leaf do not eat into the leaf nearly so deeply as in the rowan. Nor, in contrast with the rowan, is the maple a bush-like tree, but rather a true tree with trunk, crown and roots.

In addition the Norway maple has sugary sap, which was traditionally harvested by Native Americans. There is now a whole industry in maple syrup, which is added to many North American dishes such as pancakes.

We have already said that everything sugary has a tendency to turn dark. The rowan is not sugary and this is why the light can enter deeply into the plant through its feathery qualities. This isn't the case with the maple. Its tips or drips merely indicate an attempt to go in this direction. In place of this one finds its sweetness in the colouring leaves in autumn. The rowan leaves turn a deep, coral red when they fall, whereas the maple leaf is already turning brown when it falls. This shows that it contains something dark or sweet.

In Europe maple syrups were rarely used because Europeans held back from this dark ingredient. European maples also don't have such quantities of syrup as the North American tree.

We find a flight principle in the seeds of the maple, which look like a bird's spreading wings. They fly very well, but their swelling hub also bears a marked tendency towards weight and gravity. In the maple you find a very strong duality between light and dark — much more than in the rowan, which absorbs the light to a far greater degree.

Lightness and weight

WW: Who are you?

Crissie: I am the tender of the European maples. I wholeheartedly agree with what Theabrox said about us.

WW: The maple is a medium-sized tree and its crown is usually egg shaped. What does this form tell us?

Crissie: On the one hand it shows the tendency to lightness, but on the other, in the lower part of the egg form, it shows weight which again has a drop-like quality. One can see the egg as a falling drop. I tend towards heaviness, or fluid qualities.

WW: Your trunk is remarkably straight. What does this express?

Crissie: My trunk expresses an upright force, which is necessary for me to mediate my beautiful light colouration. To do this I have to overcome my other aspect, of gravity and fluid. There is always this counterplay in me — heavy, fluid nature and yet light-filled.

WW: When one snaps off a maple twig or leaf, a milky sap is exuded. What is the significance of this?

Crissie: That isn't the same sap that is exuded from the trunk, but a variant of it. It's more watery in the leaf, whereas the fluid in the trunk is the tree's blood. In the trunk the fluid element is overcome, whereas in the leaves it's more like the trapping of light within the fluid.

Sap rises in spring

WW: Is it bad for you when people cut slits in your trunks and collect the sap?

Crissie: No, this sacrifice is inherent in my gesture. I am glad to give away fluid. You can see from the shape of my leaf that I am pleased to dispense drops. But it is bad for me when you humans overdo it. In the past the Native Americans knew — as do those who cultivate me carefully and show me proper care — how much sap to take from maple trees without harming me. But taking too much can harm me. I also have varying qualities depending on the time of year, for my spring sap is quite different from my autumn sap. The first is more enlivening, the second richer in vitamins. But I am always willing to share my fluids with you within due bounds.

WW: What time of year is best for tapping the most syrup?

Crissie: I have most in the spring.

WW: And then excess pressure builds up in the trunk?

Crissie: Yes, because the sap is rising. Sap rises in all plants in spring, but excess pressure builds up in me particularly.

WW: What happens then when no one taps your syrup?

Crissie: I form less of it. Climate change is a problem for me, because it alters the distribution of fluids. You cannot milk me if I have no moisture. And if less rain falls towards summer and autumn, my sap is diminished in the second half of the year. But in normal years I don't get mastitis like a cow that no one milks; I just form less sap. Now and again, though, my trunks are damaged by animals or weather conditions, and my sap simply runs out into the soil.

WW: What relationship does the maple have to other deciduous trees, for example to oaks, limes and elms?

Crissie: There are only very few elms. Many trees don't care to grow in my society because I take a great deal of fluid from the ground. That's why other trees prefer me as a single tree or in rows. I myself have fewer problems with other trees; it is they that find me a problem.

A promise to Native Americans

WW: Does the maple also have mythological significance?

Crissie: In Native American culture there is a legend about the maple, which says that its golden-coloured leaves in autumn are a promise to the people that the sun and the spring will return next year; therefore they should not despair during the forthcoming winter. By growing golden the maple shows that nature is only slumbering temporarily in winter.

WW: Here in Europe it is said that the maple calms easily-frightened people if they rest under it for a few minutes each day. It is also thought to be a tree for optimists and for inducing good moods. Is there some truth in this?

Crissie: There's a great deal of truth in it. I've already spoken of hope for the forthcoming year and the sun's return. The autumn's beautiful colours show this hope for next spring. By not over-accentuating either the watery or light aspects — unlike the rowan, which has almost only a light aspect — I bring a certain equilibrium to those in whom both constituents have become disordered, such as people suffering from depression or stress. This happens either when they study me with interest or spend a while in my aura. Being close to a maple can have a stabilizing effect on people, primarily because I bring water and light into equilibrium.

WW: Does it mean anything to you to be depicted on a country's flag?

Crissie: It pleases me. I also try to endow Canada with my being and to promote non-commercial use of the maple. I also try to spread well with my flying seeds, which ensure that I can flourish everywhere.

WW: What importance does maple wood have?

Crissie: It is not a very hard wood, but a good resinous wood. It is also good when used in centres where people with mental health issues are cared for. Such people should try to surround themselves with maple or use objects made of maple wood, for this will restore their equanimity.

WW: Which human quality corresponds to the maple?

Crissie: Volatility, as expressed in the two phrases: over the moon and down in the dumps.

The Sycamore

Acer pseudoplatanus

WW: What can be said about the sycamore's leaves?

Theabrox: The sycamore is a European maple, but it's striking that the leaves scarcely have this drop shape — no roundness between the tips. This shows that sugar extraction does not have such importance in Europe; this tree is unable to let its sap flow in this way. The sycamore tends to form a more enclosed leaf, which is also five-lobed, though three-lobed in older trees, with two small interior lobes. This shows that the sycamore's leaves are not so devoted to capturing light. Instead it is able to grow at great altitudes. But it does not establish the same equilibrium between water and light as the maple, and it does not turn so golden and red in autumn.

WW: But the leaf stems turn red. Why is that so?

Theabrox: The leaf stems are very long. The leaves are pushed

a very long way out so that the red colour cannot reach them. If the stems were shorter, the autumn colours could run into the leaves themselves. The sycamore's devotion to light is not expressed in the leaf but in the stem instead.

Black spots

WW: Why are sycamore leaves often covered in black spots?
Theabrox: They can become very black, especially after falling.
WW: Why is this so?
Theabrox: This is because the light constituent evaporates and
   the watery aspect passes into putrefaction. When the light
   quality separates out and only the dark remains, you have
   all the sycamore's heavy components visible before you. The
   sycamore leaf slowly disintegrates after turning red and falling
— it becomes a dark sludge.

WW: Actually I didn't mean the general
disintegrative tendency of sycamore
leaves but specifically the dark spots
that appear on some leaves.

Theabrox: That's a disease: a fungal
infection that attacks sycamores. The
sycamore always tries to maintain equilibrium between water
and light. This spot disease is due to a preponderance of one
of the components — moisture, cold, warmth etc. It happens
when a certain symptom of disease interferes with the water-
related task. Similarly, increasing levels of this disease are an
aspect of climate change.

WW: Why is the bark of the sycamore often covered in mosses and
   small fungi?
Theabrox: Because, as we already saw with the leaf, the sycamore
   has a much stronger tendency towards the wet element than
   the maple for instance. That's why mosses, fungi and lichens
   grow well on sycamore trunks. The silver maple, in contrast, has a
   much more pronounced tendency towards capturing the light. It is
   astonishing that as yet scarcely any detailed studies of the forms of
   these leaves have been undertaken.

WW: Why does the bark of older trees peel off in scales?
Theabrox: If the bark's fungal infestation grows excessive, and becomes
   alien to the tree, the tree begins to shed its bark. This is another
   attempt to counteract moisture, and is the reason why sycamores
   — particularly old trees — shed their bark at certain periods.

More oriented towards light

The sycamore grows towards the light much more than the maple. The latter grows, for instance, in the Canadian plains, whereas the sycamore mostly grows at much higher altitudes. That is why it doesn't have to make such an effort, for example, in its leaf-shape, to receive light; on mountain slopes it quite naturally receives a greater influx of light. This is also why it can bring the wet element to expression more strongly within itself. Sycamores growing at lower heights have to work a lot harder to overcome moisture.

Open to the astral

WW: What happens when the sycamore's blossoms are pollinated by bees and flies?
Theabrox: Rowan and sycamore blossoms have some things in common. If a creature flies to a sycamore flower, an astral being approaches an etheric one. The tree is almost entirely an etheric being. Bees and flies naturally bear a strong 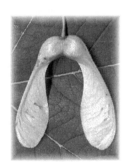 astrality. The moment a bee or fly lands on a sycamore blossom — this applies to all trees — the tree becomes aware of another dimension. The tree makes contact with another realm of spiritual activity, which does not correspond with its usual orientation.

It is similar to when you, a human, begin to engage with animals. At this moment animals experience something spiritually oriented coming towards them, which can also direct and guide them. Similarly, at pollination, trees perceive that there are other worlds besides the etheric, and they begin, very tentatively, to develop towards them. The process of pollination initiates development in trees.

WW: What happens when sycamore seeds are spread on the wind?
Theabrox: When the sycamore releases its seeds it has, basically,

fulfilled its task and does not mourn their loss. The seed passes beyond the tree's dominion and close proximity. This is not a noticeably transforming process such as you find in animal reproduction. Pollination and seed formation are a further development, in which the salamanders also collaborate as further spiritual presence. Salamanders correspond etherically to human beings. When the sycamore releases its seeds it no longer has any awareness of them. The sycamore is deeply persuaded — and you can see this in the red coloration of its leaves, or at least its leaf stalks — that another spring will come.

WW: Why is sycamore wood good for musical instruments such as guitars or violins?

Theabrox: The sycamore grows very slowly in the mountains, and there its watery components do not disturb it. At the same time the wood is very much formed by cold winds and strong light, and it bears a strong affinity with the light. This means it can resonate very well. Tones arise between water and light, and this is why the sycamore is, as it were, predestined for making instruments. The musical tone is connected with sound ether and is at the same time a dematerialized fluid. And a tree that is very close to these processes naturally gives ideal wood for making musical instruments.

The Field Maple

Acer campestre

WW: The field maple is an almost bush-like tree, which does not grow as tall as other types of maple. Its leaves are often five-lobed but they don't have pointed tips like the Norway maple. What does this tell us?

Theabrox: Some leaves are also three-lobed, with only a hint of  the two lower lobes on either side. The field maple is a rather child-like form of the maple. The shape of the leaf is midway between the sycamore and the Norway maple, and bears their tendencies in miniature form. It does not grow in woods but prefers sunlit places, and its orientation towards the light is expressed in the large lobes of the leaves. It is more of a hedge and bush kind of plant.

WW: Why are there so many different types of maple, which are sometimes barely distinguishable?

Theabrox: This lies in their nature. A tree that seeks to balance feeling and thinking needs to form a different variety for every region of the earth.

Thinking, feeling and will are a little different in every region of the globe. A person in India feels differently from someone in the Congo. It is the same with human thinking in different regions. Light corresponds to thinking, water to feeling. The maple embodies the interaction of these two constituents, and since people on earth are very different, the maple varieties must adapt accordingly.

The Silver Maple

Acer saccharinum

WW: What can you tell me about the silver maple, which is indigenous to North America, but which we also find in Europe as an ornamental tree in parks? What is characteristic of this tree?

Crissie: This tree is very decorative, which is why people like planting it in parks. The leaves usually show the five-lobed aspect very clearly. You can also see that they embody a strong light affinity, and therefore a strong relationship to dryness. Since the dry aspect predominates, the silver maple has less sap and is not so useful as source of syrup.

WW: Why are the leaves so deeply cleft and serrated?

Crissie: This is because light penetrates them so strongly. Some of the indentations are so deep that little curves arise between the lobes, whereas the field maple shows no such curves. In contrast, the silver maple's leaves are almost saw-toothed, which is a sign — as in the rowan — that light elements exert a greater influence on this tree than watery constituents. This means that the silver maple is much drier as a tree. It does not make proper syrup, which in turn means that the dark quality of weight has been dispelled from this tree.

WW: If you examine the leaves of the silver maple they look silvery-white on their underside. Why is this?

Crissie: This protects them against drying out too much. The silver reflects light. It is similar with poplar trees and aspens: then you really see the whole tree twinkle. By doing so the silver maple, despite its light-affinity, dispels some of the light. People regard the silver maple as a very pretty tree. I don't have so much of a problem with moisture but must instead protect myself from excess, shimmering light.

The Black Alder

Alnus glutinosa

WW: Hello Ella.

Ella: Hello Wolfgang.

WW: Tell me something about you. What kind of a tree are you?

Ella: I like having wet feet. I can grow well in water. My wood is interesting because when exposed to air it turns reddish orange.

WW: Why?

Ella: It rusts because we contain a lot of iron; this looks lovely and points to my connection with Jupiter. Jupiter's colour is yellowy orange.

WW: Why do you like growing in wet places?

Ella: Trees also have to grow in wet places.

WW: Sure, but other trees could grow in damp places. Why do you in particular grow there?

Ella: Because that's how the spirits of creation made me, to grow in wet places. I am capable of coping with both dry and damp conditions. I also like being in proximity to humans and close to soggy meadows, because then I can draw the moisture from them. My root system can do this.

An island by nature

WW: Can you tell us something about your roots? How do you manage to grow in soggy areas and in water?

Ella: I grow in a way similar to a mangrove tree: my roots develop like sponges and are not as smooth or distinct as the roots of most trees. What I have is more like a net of roots. I form a kind of dish upon which I stand. I am not invariably a single-trunk tree but am more like an island by nature — round like my leaves — and on this island stand several trunks, which all belong to my alder being.

Of course you can force an alder to be a single tree, but in a marshy woodland area it is common for alders to form a kind of island tree-group. In fierce storms the whole root-dish can be upturned, and you will see that the roots don't penetrate the earth very deeply as individual fibres, but stand on the dish, which sits like a sponge on the marshy or moist ground. My roots can float and also transport air. We alders are guardian trees protecting etheric beings.

WW: Where alders grow in larger numbers — in swampy areas, for instance in the Spreewald in Germany — you can also find large numbers of rare and endangered plants and animals.

Ella: Yes, and a good thing too.

WW: What is the connection? Do alders offer some kind of protection for these rare plants and creatures?

Ella: Spreewald is a special area. In the alder thickets a special connection exists between alders and etheric beings; the elves and alders have a very intimate connection. Sick trees come time and again to the alder tree swamp to Kollii, the One From the Marsh, to be cared for. We alders have the capacity to form communities. Whoever we accept into our community is then in a protected sphere with us. This might be humans and animals, but also equally plants or tree beings. Most etheric beings like being in our proximity, and a visible sign of this are the shrouds of mist that tend to hover over alder swamps. The protective spheres that form are stronger with larger numbers of alders. We don't tend to grow in the mountains, but rather in the plains of northern Europe, and you can find small alder swamps everywhere there.

WW: The black alder provides a habitat for around 150 species of insects — 75 of which are types of butterfly — several dozen birds, and over 70 species of fungus. Is this also connected with a healing? Why are large numbers of butterflies drawn to alders?

Ella: Butterflies are blossoms that have released themselves from the soil and are attracted to the etheric beings that are present with us. We alders protect the etheric beings. Butterflies feel that they are related to etheric beings, and birds feel something similar. Birds also find themselves drawn to human thoughts, and in their great migrations, birds to some extent are akin to the thoughts of human beings. In a similar way butterflies are attracted to the etheric beings dwelling in the alders' proximity. Healthy etheric beings reside particularly in the areas surrounding alders, for hardly any such beings are left in towns and cities. Wherever there are alders, etheric beings grow healthy, and therefore butterflies and other insects fly there. Everything that is trying to become more vital and healthy, and can fly, streams towards the alders. Creatures that cannot fly of course find it harder to reach us.

WW: Why does the alder not grow very old — 120 years at most?

Ella: Because we keep getting young again. You should not think of us as a trunk tree such as an oak. Instead we keep forming our island: the older alders fall down while the younger ones take their place. Of course there are also individual alders, but the black alders have this communal tendency.

WW: Why is the bark of the black alder very dark, almost black?

Ella: The dark colour comes from the moist, damp areas where we grow, and from the fact that the moisture rises up through the trunk. If you dry the bark out it becomes grey.

The drop has landed

WW: The leaves of the black alder tend to be round and have no pointed tip, but rather a dint at the end. Why is this?

Ella: The drop has landed.

WW: What does this mean?

Ella: Our leaves are almost circular and very closely related to the element of water. Their shape reflects the form of a drop. They are not floppy and soft, however, but have a certain resilience. Their flattened and dinted ends show that the drop has landed on the ground and become flattened.

While Maple and sycamore trees engage with light and moisture, the alder engages with the earth and moisture. This also causes the dark bark coloration, showing that moisture rises upwards from below, and the island formation with its special type of roots which, within their mesh, naturally grasp soil. It is necessary that our root-mesh grasps hold of earth, especially when we grow in flowing water, otherwise the soil would be washed away. This is all hinted at in the shape of the leaf. The wet element has landed on the ground and tries with its two, horn-like tips (which can often be seen) to penetrate the earth and establish itself there.

Female catkins

WW: What can you tell me about the alder catkins?

Ella: There are two different forms, the so-called female and male catkins. Our catkins are not so velvety as willow catkins, but they are very loose in consistency. Our female catkins are full of pollen. If you shake an alder twig bearing catkins, a bright green cloud will form. The so-called male catkins are a great deal smaller and look like small buds. All catkin-bearing trees are more youthful trees. Catkins embody nature's playful trait.

Male catkins

WW: The alder is in grave danger today, and has

been dying out for a good ten years now. Can you say anything about this?

Ella: They're not dying here.

Verena Staël von Holstein: She's looking into it.

Ella: When alders die it means that the wet element has grown too strong.

WW: It is said to be due to a fungal organism, whose spores actively spread in water and penetrate the alders so they die from the roots upwards. What are the causes of this disease?

Ella: When a pest spreads it means that a beneficial organism is lacking and that circumstances are changing radically and one-sidedly. In consequence the tree tenders decide that some trees must withdraw from certain areas. You would have to ask such a tree tender exactly why the alders must withdraw.

WW: For the alder this means that its natural habitat — water — becomes its greatest threat.

Marsh beings

Since we're speaking about alders in relation to marshy areas, perhaps we should talk a little about the nature of a marsh or swamp. What is the nature of the marsh, Kollii?

Kollii: Hello, I've often told you this.

WW: But it would still be very good if you could say a few words about it at this point.

Kollii: There are various kinds of marsh: upland moors, fens and peat bogs. The interesting thing about such areas is that things only partially rot in them. If all plants in the marshes rotted away completely, it would form humus. This does not happen, but instead peat forms; and this shows that the rotting process is not completed. An upland moor is a former fen that has dried out in the course of time, where you get upland moor plants. Another condition for a marsh is that water cannot flow away from it, that standing pools form. Such standing pools mean that all organic substances — leaves, trees and also dead animals — are enclosed and kept away from the air. When plant material is sealed off from the air, it does not rot but just gets waterlogged.

When a marsh is formed, special beings develop in it. As you know, the beings who regulate processes of dying tend to be assigned to the descending or degenerate spirits. Nevertheless these beings are very important, because without them we would be swamped in waste. But since a lack of oxygen — which cannot get through to organic materials in the marsh because of the standing water — means that rotting does not take place fully in marshes, these beings assigned to degenerate energies transform themselves and become brighter again. And so the typical marsh beings arise: dark beings that cannot remain as dark as they should be if they were to accomplish their work properly.

WW: Can you explain this in a little more detail?

Kollii: These are transformed beings of putrefaction, which facilitate rotting and decomposition. Such beings are connected with or arise from death processes. They are needed to allow the etheric to leave the corpses of humans, animals and plants, and to re-integrate them with the earth's great body. When this process of disintegration is disturbed through a lack of oxygen, the beings who would normally undertake it are transformed. They can no longer complete their work as envisaged. This means that they transform their etheric nature. Spiritual beings in the etheric realm are expressions of the will of hierarchical beings. But if this will cannot work in its intended way, it must transform.

The incomplete rotting process is caused by the lack of oxygen. Oxygen is the bearer of all life, and thus of the etheric.

Unchanging stasis, neither life nor death

If oxygen as life-bearer is lacking, all processes of transformation are disrupted. If these 'death beings' cannot work properly, and if, at the same time, life cannot penetrate to them, a sphere is formed in which there is neither life nor death. All processes in the marshes unfold as though time is suspended. All beings are normally subject to change, but the moment that stasis holds sway, the changes in beings dwelling there cease.

This gives the marshes and the beings living in them a special character: in a sense the marshes provide a realm of non-time. This has a remarkable, and in many cases alarming, effect on people. In former times, and as part of the rites practised in northern lands, criminals were driven into the marshes; if they survived they were regarded as innocent. Such people were forced to confront non-time — the undead and the unliving, neither one thing nor another. If they could endure this and emerge from the marshes, they were no longer thought to be guilty.

Fen fires or will-o'-the-wisps

WW: What are will-o'-the-wisps?

Kollii: The souls of the dead who do not find their way into the world of spirit yet still search for it desperately. They can dwell more easily in marshy areas since time there is held in stasis, and that's why they gather there. Not all such souls are marsh-like, but sadly there are still such souls there.

WW: Are there connections between the alders, the marshes and these will-o'-the-wisps?

Kollii: Alders are open-hearted beings which protect everything

Bog cotton

that approaches them with a plea for help. That is why they offer a safe space for these beings, who are paralyzed and unable to advance. But alders only grow at the edges of the marsh, and are not an actual marsh plant. Bushes and marsh birch grow directly in the marshes, and of course also bog cotton and suchlike.

WW: Wet alder leaves also look like will-o'-the-wisps in the dark, and people of olden times thought that's what they were when they saw them. Wet alder leaves are not will-o'-the-wisps, but is there any connection between these two things?

Kollii: Many things can rightly be explained in a logical and rational way. On the other hand, one can certainly assume that there are will-o'-the-wisps in the marshes and that these are not just reflections from alder leaves. Both are true.

People who had no peace in their lives, who were bound to certain places but could not inwardly connect with these places and so felt tormented, and who also found no religious faith, are unredeemed souls. Will-o'-the-wisps were often repulsed from the threshold after they died. There is no guardian of the threshold in the marshes.

WW: What does this mean?

Kollii: No guardian can be there, for no transition is possible and time stands still.

WW: If someone goes into the marshes today and spends a few hours there, how will this affect him?

Kollii: It will affect him psychologically in particular. Since time does not run its course there, a person will try to gain some grasp somehow, and is, more or less unconsciously, schooling his higher senses. He will try to reach into realms beyond the outward senses. Human nature cannot endure stasis, rigidity, and will try to acquire other impressions. If someone can endure this and is able to have supersensible perceptions, it will be beneficial to spend some hours in the marshes.

WW: Many thanks.

Kollii: There's still a great deal we could say.

Venice

WW: Ella, let's turn back to you. There is a city built on alder stakes, called Venice. What is the effect on a city when large areas of it are supported in this way?

Ella: This is why there's a special carnival in Venice and people there can contact all kinds of supersensible figures. The Venetians are better placed to see that there are more things between heaven and earth than ordinary earthly consciousness acknowledges. You can see this in Venice in all sorts of art forms, for instance in its masks. This city has a feel for supersensible images, and at the same time it has a timeless quality, because the alder stakes give it a somewhat marsh-like character. Those who visit Venice will find that time has stopped there to some degree. This is caused by the alders beneath the houses of Venice, which make the city into a marsh. Nevertheless the city is slowly sinking.

The Grey Alder

Alnus incana

WW: What is the difference between the black and grey alder?

Ella: Unlike the black alder, whose trunks tend to be black, the grey alders are grey. They have much less affinity with water, as you can see clearly in the shape of the leaf: it is not so flattened at the tip but still has a point, and the underside of the leaf is a good deal greyer.

WW: The leaves of the grey alder are much smaller; they are coarse and finely serrated. What kind of nature does this express?

Ella: The tree tries to catch sylphs by this means. The grey alder is the only alder which strives towards the sylphs: it does so a good deal in alder terms, but only a little compared with other trees. The fine serrations are an attempt to become more pinnate, to approach dryness. This tree is not so full of moisture, nor does it like growing in water. But it is, nevertheless, a real alder; the grey alder, too, can create protective spaces.

WW: And what significance is there in the blue-ish and hairy underside of the leaves?

Ella: The hairy underside is another attempt to work its way into the airy element and grasp hold of it. The lighter colour of the underside of the leaf is more oriented towards the light. You can that this alder has slightly altered its form to give itself up more to qualities of air and sylph-hood. It is really quite simple — you humans need to look at trees with more careful attention.

The helping and protecting gesture

WW: What human quality corresponds to the alder?

Verena Staël von Holstein: She's searching for words. Motherly qualities have occurred to her, but that isn't quite right.

Ella: It is more like the image of a female herb gatherer and herbalist. The alder has something very feminine, a quality that draws you. But it is not the quality of an old woman; that would not be right. Really she has the protective, caring gesture of a child's nursemaid. This fits best: a nursemaid who always has a comforting word and in whose arms one can take refuge — but not the birth mother. She has a motherly, caring and protective quality, and also perhaps a touch of the witch.

WW: Is there anything else you would like to say about the alder?

Ella: No, not really.

Theabrox: We haven't yet really spoken about its wood. As well as being reddish it shrinks relatively little. It is not very tough but has an interesting capacity: when this wood is standing in water it takes a very long time to rot. It fills with the water it absorbs and becomes almost indestructible — otherwise Venice would long since have gone under. A special capacity of alder wood, therefore, is its suitability for underwater construction. A good oak can do this too, but it must first be stored a long time in water. The alder has this capacity immediately.

Horse chestnut

The Common Horse Chestnut

Aesculus hippocastum

WW: Hello Petra

Petra: Hello Wolfgang

WW: The horse chestnut is a very big tree ...

Petra: But we start small ...

WW: ... and it forms a dense, broad crown. What is expressed in the nature of this tree?

Petra: The first thing that people recall when they think about the horse chestnut is the deep shade it casts. Scarcely any other tree grows large and dense enough to cast such a broad, dark shadow.

WW: Although the horse chestnut needs so much light.

Petra: Exactly. You don't get horse chestnut woods either, or very rarely. Horse chestnuts tend to prefer being solitary trees. But you have often planted avenues of us in your villages and towns.

Stability is important for us

What is our nature? At first sight the horse chestnut doesn't look very different from other trees. But if you look more carefully you will see that a horse chestnut has no fine branches, no filigree network of twigs. It has relatively thick branches, the thinnest of which are finger-thick shoots growing from the larger boughs, with minimal branchings. The horse chestnut has very large, candle-like blossoms. These candles secrete a great deal of nectar, sometimes even dripping with it. Only the lime tree produces more. Our large, five- to seven-fingered leaves are striking: these are soft and lobed, and very numerous on the tree. It is also noticeable that we let our leaves fall in autumn more or less at the same time. Horse chestnut leaves can really rain down.

WW: Let's go back over some of the details.

The trunk starts branching at a fairly low height, into several strong boughs. Why is this?

Petra: The horse chestnut has an affinity with stability, which you can also see from the fact that we tend not to form fine branches. We always need a very stable quality. A tall trunk that does not form side branches until it reaches a good height is less stable than one with a short, stocky trunk, which goes into boughs at an early stage.

It is only in our leaves that we loosen up, as the leaf has separate fingers. The leaves of the horse chestnut have a certain similarity with the human hand. All fingers grow from a single point, from a relatively short but strong stem. This means that we have a marked affinity with a stabilizing, focusing, gathering together and herding element. This is also expressed of course in our fruits, the conkers, which are not suitable for human consumption. They are not poisonous but don't taste very good to you.

The tree of seasonal rhythm

WW: The horse chestnut tree seems to embody the seasons. The large buds appear in winter, the large-fingered leaves in April, the huge, orchid-like blossoms in May, and in autumn come the prickly fruits. Is the horse chestnut a tree that tries to impress a sense of the changing seasons on the people of our latitudes?

Petra: The horse chestnut has a very marked connection with rhythm and suffers a great deal if it cannot maintain its rhythm. It needs its clearly patterned cycle of the year and at each season wishes only to do one thing at a time. In jungles, in contrast, there are trees on which one branch is wilting, another is bearing blossoms, and yet another is fruiting — all at the same time. The horse chestnut cannot do this. We need very clear divisions. This rigidity and clarity of form manifests right into the twigs and leaves. The leaves' individual fingers have distinct edges and do not easily rot away.

WW: Why are the buds so sticky?

Petra: So that life can emerge from them. The formative strength of our tree means that we tend to form life too strongly, and at the moment of blossoming we pour out what is living in us, but it finds difficulty in expressing itself due to the strong formative quality. That is why the bud is so sticky and attracts all kinds of insects. It is similar with our blossoms, which have varying colours depending on the variety of tree.

WW: Why is the horse chestnut one of the first trees to come into leaf?

Petra: Because the time is right, because this belongs to the strongly rhythmic nature of our tree and because, unlike other trees, we do not produce blossoms and leaves at the same time. First we form the leaves and then we flower. If a bare horse chestnut were to blossom this would be terribly indecent. We must first clothe ourselves properly and then we flower.

In winter you see our earth element: the strong boughs that divide very little. Then in spring comes the leaf, clearly expressing the drop-shaped water element. Then come the blossoms with the light element: not at Michaelmas tide, it is true, but still in the right sequence. And then comes warmth in the formation of fruits. There is a very clear sequence here.

WW: The longest finger in the five- to seven-fingered leaves is the middle one. Why?

Petra: It is the biggest because it is the leading and orienting leaf. If you observe how a leaf grows, you will see that this finger always comes ahead of the others. That's why it is biggest: it's the chief of all the fingers on a leaf.

WW: Why do the leaves turn golden-yellow in autumn, and then later brown?

Petra: Towards the end the leaves do turn a definite brown, though this is a light brown. The individual fingers also start rolling up. We have impressed on the leaves that they must return their moisture so as to symbolize the solid element. The leaves dry out. The yellowing of the leaves in autumn is in gratitude to the light, for we live in a light-accentuating time; this is why it is also our task to express thanks to the light.

WW: Why does the trunk have such a strong and coarse scale-bark, and why does it twist so much as it grows?

Petra: The strong rhythm informing us means that we take a step onwards and upwards at every rhythmic turn, giving rise to a spiral effect. We cannot leave the location where we grow, but can only grow upwards, and this causes the twisting movement of the horse chestnut. If we didn't do this we would grow unstable.

WW: The horse chestnut is flowering ever earlier; is this connected with climate change?

Petra: Of course. This is connected with your global experiment. If you change the rhythm of the year and shift the light quality that we need at a particular time of year, we are compelled to follow. This isn't good for us, but there's nothing else we can do. And if spring grows ever shorter and summer comes ever earlier, we will have to blossom earlier and earlier, for otherwise our flowers would appear in the summer phase, and that would be unrhythmical. We can do nothing that is unrhythmical.

WW: This must be very problematic for you.

Petra: Yes indeed, because the conkers really ought to come earlier too, but we lengthen our ripening phase.

WW: You can do this?

Petra: We have to, for the conkers have to come in autumn. The disturbance of natural rhythms caused by people means that we horse chestnuts are becoming weaker and can no longer defend ourselves against the horse chestnut leaf miner (Cameraria ohridella).

We heal where forms dissolve

Nectar guide pattern

WW: The blossom consists of very beautiful, candle-like flower stalks around thirty centimetres high. Why does the horse chestnut form such a beautiful, large blossom?

Petra: These are very sturdy blossoms. They are very large because we are also very large, and therefore the size of blossom is appropriate. You have to assign to all parts of a whole what belongs to them. We have a strong, solid trunk, representing the earth. The blossom is present for the shortest period and therefore, to embody and encapsulate a great deal of light, it has to be large and stable; then the light beings are not disadvantaged. It is also our task to bear what is stable and strongly formed into all spheres, and to show that it is possible to create a connection between what is strongly formed in the fruit, and the light in the blossom and the leaf.

We horse chestnuts have the task of showing that every condition can manifest in a rhythmical, strongly-formed way. That is why horse chestnut is also used to counter tissue degeneration in you, for it brings new formative power. Wherever form is being lost, such as in the veins, where form is dissolving, we can intervene in a healing way. We really have a great deal of formative power.

WW: Each blossom consists of five creamy-white petals, the topmost two of which show a coloured spot, the so-called 'nectar guide pattern.' This spot is coloured orange or red. What is the purpose of this nectar guide?

Petra: It serves to attract insects. Some insects are not drawn to white flowers but only to the colour red, and others only to the colour yellow. Our nectar guide is yellow in the first two days, and most insects are attracted to this yellow. Then it changes colour to red, showing the bees and bumblebees that there is no nectar left. It is important for the insects to know that our yellow is not poisonous. The yellow again expresses what we express in the number five, the connection with Jupiter nature; orange-yellow points in the direction of this future state of the earth, the Jupiter embodiment.

Horse chestnut blossom is the sturdiest of all tree blossoms in our regions. Transformation of the blossom into the horse chestnut fruit takes a fairly long time, because they really only mature in autumn. The fruits' prickly case shows the tendency to protect what is solid and formed. My fruits are not as prickly as the sweet chestnut though.

They gleam before we release them

WW: Up to 10,000 conkers form in a mature horse chestnut, and weigh about 20 g each. How can a tree carry such weight?

Petra: We are stable enough to cope!

WW: Yes, but where do you draw this enormous strength from?

Petra: It is because we symbolize stability. It is true that all our fruit together weigh a great deal: not just the conkers themselves but their fleshy case as well. But just look at us: we don't have spindly branches. We form decent, thick boughs before we develop our fruit. We don't hang up our conkers on frail bits and bobs like other trees. In the tree world we are a symbol for stability on the one hand, and beauty on the other. Try to grasp that the dark shade of the horse chestnut also means it conceals beauty within. If you walk through the summer heat and encounter a horse chestnut, entering the shade and stability we represent is also a sensory experience. It is as though you were in a house, and you can find shelter for a long time under us when it's raining.

WW: What task does the prickly shell around the conker have?

Petra: It serves primarily to protect the smooth conker inside. Have you ever picked up a fresh conker and felt its wonderful texture? It gleams and shines, but this luminosity soon fades. The shell's task is to protect this solidity and beauty against premature emergence and loss. The conkers ripen for a fairly long time and not only have a prickly case outside but also a kind of pithy layer inside, allowing them to develop in ideal conditions.

WW: As children we used to take conkers still in their shells and lightly rub the green shell while dipping them in water. After a short while this produced a dark-brown, fuzzy ball ... Why do conkers have such a large white spot?

Petra: To show that we are good. The bright spot on the dark-brown conker shows our light affinity. In addition, this bright spot is the place from which a new tree can develop. For us, conkers in their shells are like jewels, gleaming in our cases before we release them.

WW: In former times no horse chestnuts existed in our latitudes. They were only brought to central Europe in 1576 with the Turks, coming by way of Vienna. The Turks brought conkers with them as horse fodder. Does this mean that the horse chestnut does not belong in our latitudes at all? Or has it by now become indigenous?

Petra: The horse chestnut has established itself very well everywhere. It does not just come from Asia Minor but also grew at the edge of the European Mediterranean. That is more or less the same kind of landscape as here in central Europe, though more southerly. As such, the horse chestnut was not so foreign, certainly not in the same way as a tree from America or Australia.

The stable, unchanging nature of the horse chestnut, and of Turkish culture at that time, both share a similar trait. The Turks did not ally themselves with the prevailing cultural impetus in central Europe, but wanted to conquer and spread their own culture. It was not an attempt to arrive in a new area and fit in, but rather to impose themselves on what was already there. The culture of the Turks, which was borne further West along with the horse chestnut, was also strongly formed; was also very military. This excessive formative impetus was extenuated by the sweet chestnut, which established itself everywhere unaided, although it does find it difficult to establish itself in the North. The horse chestnut would have arrived in our regions even without the Turks, though much later. It is well adapted to this area; you humans have also adopted much from Arabic and Turkish culture, and teach them to your children in your schools and universities, chiefly in the scientific domain.

When immoderate excess transfers to the animal world

WW: We spoke previously about the leaf miner (Cameraria ohridella). Is there anything else one can do to counteract this, apart from destroying fallen leaves?

Petra: If you restore the old rhythm to the horse chestnut it will become strong enough to resist the leaf miner. But that will be hard. One person alone cannot do it. In dry summers you can water horse chestnuts if you have sufficient water to do so. It is always good for horse chestnuts if there are people who feel respon-sible for them: this helps them to stay rhythmic. If you manage to live rhythmically yourself, and tend a horse chestnut in a rhythmic way, the tree can draw healing forces from this. But if you do tend a horse chestnut, do it rhythmically — either once a day, once a week or once a fortnight. On no account do this sporadically.

Horse chestnut leaf miner

WW: The leaf miner comes from Macedonia and was first discovered there in 1984. During the nineties it spread across Europe. This moth spreads extremely fast and up to 500,000 of them can hatch from one tree. How is it possible that such a moth breeds suddenly in such huge numbers?

Petra: It is because humans increasingly allow lack of moderation to prevail. Just think of the late-flowering black cherry. This tree spreads the American way of life through the tree world, and this outlook is accompanied by a marked lack of moderation. When this immoderate excess is transferred to the animal world, it usually expresses itself in the insect kingdom. Here the leaf miner, particularly, has become excessively numerous and is able to further harm trees because of the disruption we suffer to our natural rhythm. If we were still really healthy, the moth could not multiply so strongly, and we would keep it in check. The leaf miner did not come out of the blue in 1984 but existed before this. It was able to grow so strong because we were weakened. Climate change has not just been happening recently, but, as we can see from the leaf miner's advance, we have been suffering from it for quite a long time. Nor did CO_2 suddenly fall from the sky. Environmental stress caused by humans has increased continually in recent centuries.

WW: There are other pests affecting the horse chestnut, mostly natural ones, such as the oyster mushroom that causes white rot, and the sulphur shelf or chicken-of-the-woods, which causes brown rot. Are these types of fungus very harmful to the horse chestnut?

Petra: We have lived with them for centuries or even millennia, but here too something similar is occurring. The weaker we become, the more harmful they are for us. Our weakness is the problem. Just look at it from this perspective and you will understand.

WW: Why is it so difficult to work horse chestnut wood?

Petra: Because it adheres to the principle of extreme formation right into the smallest detail. If you want to work with this wood, it is very hard to alter its form; this is at odds with our inmost nature.

Our healing, formative power might disappear

WW: Adding horse chestnut extract to bath water aids circulation in venous disorders. This is an illness of our times, which has arisen because people no longer move enough. Is it true that, through their conduct today — their lack of flexibility and movement in thinking — people are making sick the tree that might heal them?

Petra: No, that is an exaggeration. And sadly it's true that even mentally vibrant people get varicose veins: one shouldn't see this in too narrow a way. Yet there is some truth in what you say. I'd like to stress that if we continue to grow weaker, for instance through increasing attack by leaf miners, our healing force will diminish and fade. This is a simple fact. Only you humans can do something about it. On the other hand we could do something about it too, but then something quite different would happen; it would fundamentally change our nature and we would no longer be horse chestnuts.

WW: What would you be?

Petra: Whatever we became — but we would no longer be horse chestnuts. Then we would have a different healing force.

WW: In Bach flower remedies your buds are used to help people who find it difficult to learn from their own mistakes. Is there something in this?

Petra: Such people are inwardly stable and rigid in a certain sense. They are horse chestnut-like, but in a kind of distorted way, taking horse chestnut nature into the wrong area. That is why we can help these people with our buds.

WW: Is there a human quality that corresponds to the horse chestnut?

Petra: Inner formative force.

The Sweet or Edible Chestnut

Castanea sativa

WW: In many ways the sweet chestnut appears to have a very hostile form, for instance, the edges of its leaves are jagged and toothed and have small spines. Why is this?

Petra: The leaves of the sweet chestnut are quite different from mine, and without knowing, it is not obvious that they are the leaves of a chestnut at all. The sweet chestnut's problem is that its fruits are edible for human beings. This is why it protects itself with an exterior that seems so hostile — both in the serrations of its leaves and the spiky spines of its shells, which protect the fruits. The edible chestnut is much more on guard than I am. This saw-tooth principle is much more marked in its leaves. Nevertheless it also has a pronounced sturdiness. The trees are large and stable. Their shape is less rectangular than the horse chestnut and instead grows narrower as it rises. The sweet chestnut tries to protect its fruit

with its strong formative principle. You can even survive on sweet chestnuts, which are highly nutritious. They resemble bread, and can serve humans as a staple food.

WW: Before potatoes arrived in Europe, the sweet chestnut was known as poor man's bread.

Petra: Precisely. This is why the tree has armed itself so vigorously, right into the shape of its leaves. It is relatively sensitive to frost and mostly grows in more protected places. It doesn't like standing alone in a field where the wind can lash it. It really prefers more southerly, sunny conditions. Sweet chestnuts like growing in graveyards and similar protected places.

WW: What happens to a chestnut when you roast it? How does it change?

Petra: The starch is transformed from a raw, slippery, moist substance into a floury one. Something similar happens with bread: first the dough is slippery but the heat dries and changes it. The starch is transformed into a more digestible substance. In principle it is the same with the chestnut. We really are like bread. Through baking, or roasting in the case of the chestnut, the starch becomes more open-textured so that humans can better digest them and convert them into sugar. The chestnut is fairly sweet and this means it has a certain affinity with love and longing.

WW: Why is the bark of older trees so spiralling and fissured?

Petra: We already discussed the spiral form when speaking of me. The crevices are due to the bark of the sweet chestnut absorbing forces which are not given to me, and which are connected with the good taste of the chestnut. In a certain sense this tree breathes through its bark, and this constitutes the chestnut's pleasant taste.

WW: What human quality corresponds to the sweet chestnut?

Petra: Defensive inner stability and immunity from attack.

Great Poplar

The Poplar

Populus

Black poplar

WW: There are many types of poplar, mainly because many were bred in recent centuries. Is there a poplar being?

Gunilla: Good evening Wolfgang. You've often walked past me.

WW: Good evening Gunilla. There are various types of you. The black poplar has now almost died out but many others have not. What can you tell me about poplar nature?

Gunilla: The nature of the poplar is expressed in the incredible capacity of its leaves to move. You can always recognize a poplar by the whirring movement of its leaves. We can grow into fairly mighty trees and often stand together in large numbers. Poplars, especially black poplars, often stand beside rivers and can also survive floods. Poplar nature is expressed in its whispering, and our leaves give us a certain speaking ability. We really speak. Have you ever stood under a poplar and listened to it whispering? It sounds like faraway human speech, which you can't quite understand. Sometimes people compare us with gossiping old ladies.

Black poplar leaf

We are trees of the angels

Our wood is soft and we are tall trees. We have a great capacity for dynamic activity right into our foliage, and we enter into vibrant interplay with the air. As soon as a poplar's leaves move it is communicating with the sylphs. We have a deep devotion to

Leaf of the white (silver) poplar

sylphs and they, too, enjoy dwelling in our proximity. We are the trees that most actively relate to sylphs. Birches can do this too, but intense capacity for communication with the sylphs is our speciality.

On Old Sun matter was not as yet any denser than today's gases. At the end of the Old Sun period, the angels found their heirs in the sylphs in the etheric world; and thus you can say that in our conversations we communicate neither with humans, nor with birds, but with angels.

Every person has an angel, and besides these there are others. These angel beings are really closer to us than human beings. The poplar is really the tree of the angels.

WW: And when your leaves flutter strongly on summer days, and this gives an outward coolness, is this an inner conversation with the angels?

Gunilla: Certainly. They flutter with the least breeze. When poplars die, then angels withdraw.

Cottonwool-like fruits

WW: What can you say about the fruits of the poplar — the many thick white hairs which fall like cottonwool tufts from poplars, as if it were snowing in June? Why does the poplar produce

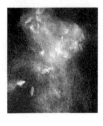

such tufts?

Gunilla: This is our attempt to depict sylph nature in the physical world. If sylphs materialized then you would see something like these puffs of cottonwool: that is our image of the sylphs, which we transpose into white clusters. Just as the angels pour their wisdom over humanity from supersensible vessels, so we pour our cotton-like fruits over the earth to tell humans about angels.

WW: What can you say about the poplar's wood?

Gunilla: Our wood is very soft and is not used very often, except for packaging.

WW: When the seeds of the poplar are released they have to find suitable soil within a few days, or be soaked in rain or dew, otherwise they lose their capacity to germinate. Why is this?

Gunilla: Because they are not earthly enough to stay longer with matter: they have simply entered matter temporarily, and so they cannot stay within it for long. We are trees of the angels and not wholly visible. That's why our wood is so soft, and everything we depict within matter is merely our material aspect. That's why our leaves are so full of movement.

WW: This is probably also why the poplar's roots sometimes grow on the earth's surface rather than delving deeply into it.

Gunilla: Precisely. That's why we poplars are not very stable and fall more easily during storms. We are one of the most etheric trees and have not fully entered matter.

WW: Why do poplars need a certain warmth and are therefore hardly found in Scandinavia?

Gunilla: Our substance has not entered very far into ahrimanic hardening. We must therefore stand more within a supersensible current of warmth than other trees. Birches, in contrast, which have a similar movement dynamic to us, can endure severe cold. We cannot because we are very much heavenly offspring.

WW: Does this mean the poplar is a weak tree?

Gunilla: You can't really say that. The poplar is just a less earthly tree.

WW: Why do birds like nesting in poplars?

Gunilla: This is connected with the sylph character of our tree. Birds and sylphs have a great deal to do with each other, even though there is not equal enthusiasm on both sides. It's true that Steiner says sylphs nestle up to birds. They do nestle up, but sometimes without the greatest enthusiasm. For the sylphs, birds embody flesh-grown thoughts a little too much. Birds like sitting in poplars because they also act in the transitional sphere between matter and spirit. Birds are still very close to the world of spirit. The birds' element is the air, and we poplars are the trees that most closely correspond to air.

WW: Why do cattle, sheep and horses like eating poplar twigs? Horses even eat poplar bark.

Gunilla: This also expresses a longing for the world of spirit or a memory of their spiritual home. These animals usually like grazing trees, however; lime tree leaves are also a very good food for them. But poplar foliage gives creatures a spiritual quality, in addition to purely physical nutrition.

WW: Poplars are highly resistant to heavy metals and salts in cities. Why is this?

Gunilla: That's quite simply due to our intrinsic nature. We don't get near to the level of heavy metals, and therefore they can't affect us much. It's true that they lodge in our leaves and wood, but they don't affect us in the sense of poisoning us. It is similar to you swallowing a handful of sand. This sand is then in you, but comes out again undigested without causing you great harm.

We dissolve carbon dioxide

WW: Does this mean poplars can detoxify soils contaminated with heavy metals?

Gunilla: In a certain sense, yes. But when heavy metals lodge in our leaves and the leaves fall to the ground, the heavy metals return to the soil. So you would always have to remove the leaves. It's similar with heavy metals lodged in my wood, although there the process takes correspondingly longer.

We can also speak here about carbon dioxide, in other words the combination of carbon and oxygen. Oxygen is the bearer of life, while carbon bears the spiritual element. When life and spirit are connected, the living element is oxidized, to express it in chemical terms. By this means something enters which leads to the spirit being displaced. When the spirit is wrongly situated, it also brings something of its primal substance with it — and this creates the state of warmth.

But since we are trees that really grow in the world of spirit, we can manage this state of the spirit and can release and dissolve it. Here chemists will object: we dissolve, as it were, the CO_2 into spirit and life, and thus release it. This is due to the activity of angels in us.

WW: This is also correct from an external perspective: no tree can absorb so much carbon dioxide from the air as the poplar, and it therefore slows down the greenhouse effect.

Gunilla: So people plant a lot of poplars. I have nothing against this. But you humans assume that the future will occur in the future. For the world of spirit the future has already happened. This is the other concept of time, which exists in the world of spirit. Since we are trees that root in the spiritual world rather than the earthly domain, we can already be in the past as we will be needed in the future. It is difficult for you humans to think of time in these terms. Some people call this inversion, others see it as concepts of the future that must first be enlivened to release their content.

WW: Can you say anything about the future of humanity and CO_2 emissions, and whether the poplar will have greater significance in this context? Would it be any use to plant great numbers of poplars, or is that nonsense?

Gunilla: Yes and no. It is possible, but then you would really have to plant a very great number of poplars, to reduce CO_2 enough to achieve a tangible effect. You would have to turn all the forests into poplar forests — but we don't grow that quickly.

WW: Why did people in ancient times, the Romans, regard the poplar as the tree of mourning and the underworld?

Gunilla: You have to examine very carefully which poplar was meant. In those days other poplars grew, for many of the types that have been cultivated over the past 200 to 300 years did not yet exist.

People thought that the whispering poplars were the voices of the dead. In a certain respect this does correspond with spiritual reality, for some of the angel voices you can hear in the poplar are also the voices of angels adjacent to people who have died. There is therefore a connection between the voices of the dead and the poplar leaves.

WW: What human quality corresponds to the poplar?

Gunilla: Humility.

Lombardy poplar (Populus nigra italica)

The Aspen

Populus tremula

WW: Can you also say something about the aspen, the only type of poplar that also grows in forests?

Gunilla: The aspen takes the poplar's fluttering leaf movement to an extreme. The leaves tend to be round, even if their edges are serrated — the serrations also tend towards roundness. This is a shape that indicates a somewhat childlike quality. Aspens can be found throughout northern Germany. They are particularly fascinating in light winds, for it looks as though the whole tree is glittering. This is because one side  of the leaf is much lighter in colour than the other. Aspens also have very soft wood, and cannot easily be used for furniture making. Aspens are not so much dwelling places for angels as for air elementals.

Globalization is impossible without the corresponding trees

WW: Why are there so many different kinds of poplars?

Gunilla: People are different, people in different regions vary, and the angels accompanying them are also different. Since angels live in poplars and are different, different types of poplars are also required. This is similar to the various types of maple. And when globalization started and people began to travel more, the types of poplar also came closer together or were crossed — and that's why there are so many species of poplar today. Changes in the way that people live together — for example when a particular group of humans migrate elsewhere in large numbers — have an affect on the trees. The trees have to accompany them. Globalization is impossible without the corresponding trees. When people emigrate, there is also a migratory tree current which attaches itself to them.

WW: When groups of people migrate to another country and take their trees with them, and these trees are alien in the new country, do these foreign trees grow better in the new land because the humans have accompanied them?

Gunilla: Absolutely. This is particularly true of poplars.

Verena Staël von Holstein: The tree tender is here. He asks whether you wish to speak with him.

WW: Yes I do. But first I still have a few questions for Gunilla. Can you say whether the aspen is the only poplar that can or does grow in forests?

Gunilla: When the weather gets really hot the leaves of the aspen turn so that the sun shines only minimally on their leaves. In Europe I am almost the only tree that can do this, whereas many trees in the tropics can. The eucalyptus tree is especially good at this, which is why you will scarcely find any shadow beneath it in a strong sun. Poplars can also do this. The aspens can do it best because their leaves move so dynamically. Because of this the light can also fall on them from other directions so that the aspens can gather in larger numbers in an aspen wood. Poplars need a great deal of light. It is only because the aspens can swivel their light paddles to get a lot of light that they thrive in a wood. Aspens are able to ensure they don't deprive each other of light.

WW: And why do aspens have this different shape of leaf? Poplar leaves are smooth and heart-shaped while the aspens' tend to be round and have round serrations.

Gunilla: Because they are the youngest of us, and childlike qualities are hinted at in the round form. The leaves are not dentate, which is also why they can stand together in communities. They have no teeth, so they don't bite. Their tips are roundish.

The Grey Poplar

Populus canescens

WW: The grey poplar is a cross between the silver poplar and the aspen. What can you tell me about the grey poplar?

Gunilla: It is less common than the aspen. Its leaf forms almost three

lobes, and is a good deal smaller than that of the poplar. It can therefore also grow in much drier locations. The grey poplar has the dynamic leaf movementtypical of poplars, and corresponds somewhat to the melancholic type. The grey poplar is a little related to mist and fog, and tends towards the alder. This is why it has clothed itself in a related colour.

WW: It grows relatively tall and has a high-arched and round crown. Why does it grow like this?

Gunilla: This height, somewhat stooping with its overhanging roundness above, expresses the melancholic character, which informs the tree's growth.

WW: The grey poplar is meant to resist storms better than any other tree in northern Germany. Is this true?

Gunilla: It seldom falls, that's true. The roots reach almost as deep into the ground as the tree is tall. But this tree's timber is too weak for making into things like furniture.

WW: The grey poplar — I can't remember which part of it — is meant to help against laryngitis, chronic bronchitis, rheumatism and psoriasis. Is this true?

Gunilla: That's right, although the poplar is not absolutely a medicinal plant. But these talking trees can support the human being's speech organs, and therefore, understandably, they are good for the larynx and lungs. If you make an infusion from the leaves, and drink this before giving a talk, you will invoke the angel beings in your speech. Used in a homeopathic dose, the grey poplar also counteracts excessive melancholy. Poplar medicines help you to come closer to the angels. If you have a piece of poplar wood beside your bed when you go to sleep, you are doing your angel a favour. If you humans decorated or furnished your homes with different kinds of wood, you could invite various beings in.

WW: Many thanks.

Gunilla: You're welcome. Please come and see me some time.

Crown, the Tree Tender

WW: Hello Crown.

Crown via Gunilla: Here I am. Good day Wolfgang.

WW: I still remember our conversation before the Iraq war.

Crown via Gunilla: I remember, in the wind. That was a good conversation.

WW: How are you?

Crown via Gunilla: Fair to middling.

WW: Why only fair to middling?

Crown via Gunilla: Because it's been very hard to concentrate this year: climate change makes a lot of work for me, and people are getting more and more unreasonable.

WW: Why?

Cultural exchange instead of sole dominion

Crown via Gunilla: Because they don't understand globalization properly — they see it in earthly not spiritual terms.

WW: What should people do differently?

Crown via Gunilla: They should grasp that globalization does not mean a single nation ruling over all others and controlling them through information technology. Instead the cultural impetus of each nation should interact equally with all others. The economy and raw materials of single nations should not be exploited by a few, but joint actions should be taken on an equal basis. Globalization should not be understood only in an economic sense, for instance as a nation's export surplus, but as equal give and take on a level playing field, as you people put it in your funny language. This also involves trying to understand the different cultures of all countries.

We're not asking, however, that you understand every detail of these things but that you try to understand at least. You must try to understand where the different raw materials come from and how global their interconnection is. If, for instance, you stopped to reflect where large quantities of titanium come from, and why there is so much of it precisely in that location, this would be a start in understanding globalization. But I am very concerned that people here are not making such efforts, and I will go on being concerned for a long time to come.

You will run out of air

WW: How big a problem is it that trees covering an area as large as Paris are now being felled every day?

Crown via Gunilla: You have to balance this with the fact that many trees are also being planted every day, which partially redresses the problem. In Europe in the last twenty years, for instance, forest cover has increased not decreased. Nevertheless it is a catastrophe that so many trees are being felled, for you will run out of air. It is really beyond comprehension how self-destructive some of your economic interests are. The whole spiritual world is astonished that you are willing to go under for the sake of a few handfuls of dollars. When this happens the dollars in your pocket will be no use to you.

The spiritual consequences of the Iraq war

WW: I always connect you with the war in Iraq. Can you say anything about the nature of the catastrophe and what consequences were triggered by the destruction of a whole country and its culture?

Crown via Gunilla: The great problem is the place where the Iraq war occurred. This was not a young region, but involved very ancient cultural sites. A great deal of this ancient heritage was forgotten and destroyed as so many people in Iraq were uprooted by the war and its consequences. This culture will have to be resurrected quite soon — no later than the next cultural epoch.

Every cultural epoch is mirrored around the fourth post-Atlantean epoch, the time of Golgotha. The preceding epoch must find its enhanced, spirit-endowed reflection in a subsequent epoch. The third post-Atlantean epoch (the Egyptian–Babylonian time) is reflected in our current fifth epoch, and the enhancement will be easier if remnants of this earlier culture are still present on earth. Since, under the guidance of Ahriman, you have succeeded in almost entirely destroying ancient Babylonian culture, which was already struggling to survive under Islam, you will have to make huge spiritual exertions in order to re-enliven this culture before you can even begin to experience the new cultural epoch. You must not skip over the coming cultural epoch, for this is already the prevailing tendency.

The next cultural epoch will be the Russian-Iranian-Iraqi one. This next, and the sixth cultural epoch, must not fail. There is already a tendency to overleap them and go straight to the seventh post-Atlantean cultural epoch, the American. This is one of the severe consequences of the Iraq war, from a spiritual perspective. The USA today is not however the America of the seventh cultural epoch! For the seventh cultural epoch America will have to change radically. Here, through the characteristics of the trees, we are trying to harmonize things in a natural way, but this is not an easy task.

Poplar and alder

WW: We have been speaking with individual trees, with the poplar and alder. We talked with the poplar about dialogue with the angels, but also about coping with CO_2 and toxins. Do you see the poplar as a tree of the future, which ought to be planted and cultivated in greater numbers to address environmental pollution and climate change?

Crown via Gunilla: Yes, but try to let it spread by itself! You don't yet have an overview of larger areas and interconnections, though this would be fine in cities. Here you could plant it.

Elsewhere you don't really know which types of trees ought to grow. Help the poplar to spread by itself. Plant it in great numbers in cities, for it will help there a great deal. It also helps children in cities, since angels congregate around poplars. In the sixth post-Atlantean cultural epoch the poplar will incarnate more strongly. It is a tree of the future. Currently it is not entirely incarnated, although one cannot really speak of incarnation in the case of trees.

WW: Yesterday we spoke about renewed occurrence of dying alders. Water-borne spores cause the alders standing in water to die. Can you say anything about this?

Crown via Gunilla: This is happening, though not in the region where you are now. There are indeed areas where the water is so contaminated and contains these fungal spores. The alders withdraw at such places since you are, basically, killing them. Keep the water clean, and then you will resolve the problem. A way to counter this is better filtration plants and less fertilizer contamination through treating of fields. Fertilizers hugely boost the growth of these fungal spores in water. If rivers grow 'thinner' again, this will also alleviate many problems of brooks and streams, and thus of the plants growing beside them. We trees are not intended for 'fat' rivers — that is, rivers containing a high level of fertilizers.

WW: What will your future tasks be?

Crown via Gunilla: My most pressing task will be to adapt trees to climate change, and I will teach them how to cope with altered climatic conditions. Moreover I will school the forest beings, who in turn teach individual tree beings. I will also engage with tall trees — you once had that great cherry here — and discuss how they can adapt to greater dryness or also very wet periods in spring. Conversations are also needed with the water capillary beings who conduct water from streams and wet areas to the trees. Likewise with the groundwater beings, who are different again from river beings.

Problems for oaks and beeches

WW: Will climate change mean that trees indigenous to southern
   climes establish themselves more in the North?

Crown via Gunilla: Definitely, and I will have to take away some
   trees of the North. This will mean that certain types of human
   being will no longer be able to incarnate there.

WW: Which trees may die out here?

Crown via Gunilla: Not the birches, but the oaks and beeches. The
   large, classic trees in these regions will primarily be affected.
   The same thing will happen to fruit and needle trees.

WW: Many thanks.

Crown via Gunilla: My pleasure. Goodbye.

WW: Goodbye.

The London Plane

Platanus acerifolia

WW: Is there a plane tree being here?

Verena Staël von Holstein: There are no plane trees here; here comes one, though, whose name is Frank.

WW: Hello Frank.

Frank: Hello Wolfgang.

WW: You are a very special being …

Frank: I am a plane tree being; planes are special!

V Staël von Holstein: This one has a certain arrogance or pride.

WW: The name plane tree comes from the Greek and means 'wide-spreading.' Can you tell me why you have such a wide-spreading crown?

Frank: I tend to grow in warmer climates. My crown is wide-spreading and also fairly high above the ground so that those seeking shade can rest under my leaves. You will see that I'm good at casting shadows.

WW: The trunks of your tree are very striking.

Frank: Lovely, aren't they?

WW: Why does the bark peel away from your trunk in such large scales?

Frank: To keep my beauty always fresh.
WW: Surely there must be other reasons too?
Frank: Why?

Noble and refined

WW: I can't really imagine that a tree would do anything simply
for beauty's sake.

Frank: The plane is a tree that embodies
nobility and refinement. We keep shedding
our bark to ensure that it never looks old
and worn. This has the great advantage
that we keep expunging death processes.
The falling scales contain the parts of us
that have grown too hard, which we can
shed. Other trees are unable to do this. At
the same time shedding bark enables us
to cool ourselves down. Beneath the places where our bark
falls off, the wood is softer to begin with, until we shed scales
again. At these places fluid can evaporate better, thus cooling
us. This scale-shedding ability allows us to create our own
microclimate.

WW: Why is the plane tree regarded as very resistant to air
pollution?

Frank: Because planes can regularly renew themselves through
their newly forming skin.

WW: If the scales keep falling off, you would assume that the
pores beneath would get blocked by polluted air.

Frank: No, on the contrary. The pores pass their dirt to the bark
scales and the scales fall off. This frees the pores from any
blockage.

WW: Why is the bark a reddish colour inside?

Frank: Mars. I have distinct Mars aspects in me, and as such
reveal my connection with this stream of cosmic being. I ought
therefore to be your favourite tree.

We are a very aggressive tree

WW: What can you tell me about the shape of your leaves?

Frank: They reveal my protective defences, especially in the sharp points of their tips. My leaves are pretty large.

WW: There are three, five or seven tips. Why?

Frank: The number is always an odd one. All these numbers are an interior disposition in us and we can therefore express them. Most trees have various sizes of leaves but the numbers of their tips are usually constant, so they cannot express anything particular in the number of tips. In the number of leaf tips, however, we planes have an expressive capacity, which is why the number of tips varies. The number of tips is also often different in any one tree, since the leaves point in different directions of the compass. The number of leaf tips tells something about the degree of aggression. We are a very self-aware and aggressive tree.

WW: Why are surfaces of the leaves almost leathery and a shiny green, whereas the undersides are matt green with downy hairs?

Frank: We need the leatheriness because we grow mostly in hot, dry regions. Since we have such large leaves, we need to protect ourselves against excessive evaporation. The underside of the leaf, especially its downy hairs, is necessary for our own micro-climate, to trap the morning dew. Our leaves collect moisture. In the warm to hot climate in which we normally grow, such large leaves are really rather impractical. Nevertheless we need them to embody our nobility.

We are defensive like the horse chestnut

WW: Why does the plane trunk branch relatively soon, and why does it spread into branches in this way?

Frank: Again, this is to show our defensive nature and to form our great crowns, which, together with our large leaves, maintain our own internal climate.

WW: Another special characteristic of plane trees is their fruit, which hang from the branches in small spheres. What can you tell me about these fruit?

Frank: Fruit and leaves show a certain connection with the horse chestnut, even if we are considerably more sharp-tipped. We are defensive like the horse chestnut. Our fruits are fairly spiky, well-packed and have long stalks. We need these long stalks to grow beyond the large leaves, for otherwise the leaves would cover the fruits up entirely. The quality of Mars is also manifest in the armoured nature of this fruit — it is closed off, can assert itself in the world of the tree, has a certain weight. It forms little external barbs, partly because sheep and goats live in the areas in which planes grow. The fruit stick on to their coats like a burr, and can thus spread far afield.

WW: There is also an oriental plane from the Caucasus and also even from Cashmere. These planes were cross-bred with western planes from Switzerland. Have these plane trees anything to do with international relations?

Frank: Yes, of course. There are many people from these countries living with you. As has been pointed out here several times, if you accept people from such countries, you also need to cultivate the corresponding trees. If you were to do this more consciously you would also have fewer problems integrating migrants. If you include the relevant trees in your awareness in relation to migration, the kinds of migratory streams would arise as flowed to America in past centuries. Many of those who emigrated to North America also quite naturally took their trees with them. This was probably also what sustained their feeling of superiority towards the native people, whereas here people come from the South and East more as supplicants. If they brought their own trees with them, the relations between you would be easier. If governments had an official tree minister, this would be very favourable for migrants to your country.

Embracing destiny and heroism

WW: What relationship do planes have to people?

Frank: The plane is there to embody the inner hero, who stands nobly steadfast and light-filled in his place. The plane is an image of human heroism. This does not by any means relate only to outwardly heroic deeds, but above all to the inner heroism of someone who can endure opposition wherever he is, and can keep his environment pure. If, as an inner image, someone can keep his castle fully defended, clean and pure, this domain will not be taken from him.

WW: In other words, once again, a tree for the human being's inner sovereignty?

Frank: Definitely. If someone connects with the plane it strengthens his inner sovereignty — in the sense of averting attacks from without and protecting the inner self.

WW: I imagine the following: a human being stands steadfast within his destiny and accepts it, but can also, plane-like, resist attacks from without.

Frank: Absolutely, the plane is an outward embodiment of someone who consciously opposes disorder and disruption. Human beings can learn this from the plane. This is easier for people if they surround themselves with plane trees, or also, for example, if they place a piece of plane wood in their house.

WW: Why is the wood of the plane tree so hard and tough, and so difficult to split?

Frank: This is also connected with our armoured nature, as our timber is very good for making shields resistant to heavy blows. It is also well suited for palisade fences. Once you have worked the timber — which is an arduous business — the finished product will be pretty indestructible. Plane wood corresponds to the tree's character, which, in contrast to the poplar, is solidly rooted in this world. The plane is secure and stable in its steadfastness, and helps people to be secure in themselves. This comes to expression in the wood, which is not good for carving since it is not pliant and must be compelled into the desired shape. The wood is, however, of outstanding quality.

Fungal infections and egotism

WW: Although the plane tree is so resilient, it suffers from a disease. For the past few years it has been under attack from so-called massaria disease, caused by a fungus. What kind of disease is this?

Frank: Wet periods have increased recently. Conditions have often been far too moist, sustaining various kinds of fungus. The fungal infection you refer to is also promoted by over-wet springs. Everything connected with fungal infections indicates

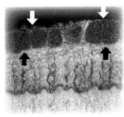

an excessively wet and earthy element, but primarily too much wetness. Since we are a tree of dry and stony regions, we find it very difficult to cope with this element, and if it reaches proportions where it is embodied in fungal entities, we become diseased and spongy, and can ultimately die.

Massaria fungus between arrows

WW: I talk with every tree about human qualities which a tree outwardly manifests. In your case we have spoken of resilience and inner resistance. In relation to these fungal spores is there anything corresponding to an inner human quality? Or are there human qualities and modes of behaviour which allow such fungal infections to arise?

Frank: As far as these types of fungus are concerned, climate change bears prime responsibility. However the cause of climate change is human egotism. In other words, increase in fungal diseases is rooted in human egotism. Human egotism extends into acquisitiveness and greed. In fact your modern culture is almost entirely based on your egotism. To the extent that you think only of yourselves and ignore both visible and invisible beings — such as trees and nature beings — entities such as these fungi will arise and further harm us.

WW: I had imagined that the connection might be more direct. If I picture to myself all that is proud, beautiful, resilient and inwardly sovereign in the plane tree, and then observe it being harmed, then I imagine a more direct link — in terms of the relationship between plane tree and human being. Is it not possible that the opposite of a human being's inner sovereignty causes such fungal infections — in other words cowardice, ignorance and lack of interest in others?

Frank: Certainly. This also includes, for example, handing responsibility for oneself to other people and to state institutions. The moment you relinquish responsibility and expect the state to do everything for you, you relinquish inner sovereignty — and promote plane tree disease. To that extent what you say is certainly right. This happens, for example, where parents demand, as they do increasingly, that nurseries and schools take on all responsibility for children instead of bringing them up themselves. But this kind of thing is a widespread tendency today. All relinquishment of responsibility due to laziness, inner lethargy and egotism belongs here; it also means that the person concerned does not grasp hold of certain areas of his own destiny.

WW: Many thanks.

Frank: You're welcome.

Linden

The Large-leaved Lime or Linden

Tilia platphyllos

WW: Hello Linda. Your name is appropriate.

Linda: Good day to you.

WW: I suspect that you are a very amenable tree.

Linda: I am above all a holy tree.

WW: Why?

Linda: Because I am dedicated to fertility.

WW: Can you say a little more?

Linda: This derives from Scandinavian tradition. In this mythology there is a goddess of fertility, called Frigga, and the lime tree is dedicated to her. I am also a very important tree in Christian tradition, for I am connected with John the Baptist. John was a vegetarian and — as people say in these parts — lived from honey and herbs. The legend tells that Christ went to the lime tree because there were fewer supplies for the bees at the height of summer, and said it should flower later so that John would still get honey. This is the secret of the late-flowering lime tree.

The lime is also the tree under which law courts were held in olden times. The lime was also often planted as memorial tree for famous people. This began before Goethe's time and ended with Udo Lindenberg. People have always connected a certain sacredness and closeness to God with the lime tree, as well as a certain demonstration of reverence. By planting a lime tree people sought to show the reverence they felt for particular famous people.

Above and beyond this there is probably no tree that has found its way so often and in such diverse ways into the names of places and inns.

Germany's oldest linden: 1200 years old

Capacity for devotion

WW: Is there a human quality which corresponds with the lime tree?

Linda: I don't have the plane tree's nobility. I have a marked practical bent, for everything I produce is useful for people.

 Lime blossoms make an excellent and very restorative tea. Lime-blossom honey is one of the best types of honey you can get. In the old days people weren't allowed to fell limes because they were so important for honey. Lime-tree

wood is one of the best woods for carving, and in contrast to plane wood is easy to shape. However this timber shrinks a good deal. Lime wood is very bright, sometimes almost white. From this you can see that we have a high moisture content, which is also an indication of our fertility. Fertility is always associated with water. And so humans can learn the capacity for usefulness from us.

WW: With all your fine qualities that sounds a little nondescript, almost insignificant.

Linda: Then call it the capacity for devotion. The capacity for devotion is the human quality which most closely corresponds to us. We give everything and retain nothing.

WW: Why is the crown of the large-leaved lime tree so broad and densely enclosed, and why does it hang down so far?

Linda: Because it bows down to human beings and is willing to devote itself. That's why it hangs down so far. It is dense and enclosed in order to do as much good as it can, for when

it is tall it bears many blossoms which form the staple of many bees' food. However, the shape of the crown is not always closed but can sometimes also be somewhat open. Actually we look the same in overall shape as a standing lime leaf. It is often the case that the shape of a leaf roughly corresponds to the shape of the tree or its crown. This is particularly true of fruit trees, for instance pear trees.

Inwardly expansive and bountiful

WW: Why does the lime grow very slowly during the first sixty years, and then faster?

Linda: Because it first needs to attain a certain height before it can unfold freely. It first has to be properly stable in its location, well rooted — this takes about sixty years — and only then can it spread itself abroad with a certain liberality. During these sixty years it has absorbed the entity of the location where it grows and can devote itself to these local beings. The linden also, of course, has a close connection with the gods of fertility and with aged venerability, which also requires that it attain a certain size. If it were small and measly it would be hard to show it reverence. People find it easier to show reverence to large trees. Large trees more easily speak to your souls. Invoking reverence is a further task of the lime tree.

WW: Reverence for what?

Linda: Reverence for fertility, for devotion, reverence for munificence. The lime is very bountiful, and really this bountifulness is a more precise description of its nature than devotion. Great people, likewise, come to your attention because they offer and give something of themselves. Bountifulness through inner expansiveness: this is what you can learn from the lime tree.

WW: People say of the lime that it takes 300 years to develop, that it stands for 300 years and takes 300 years to pass away again. Is this true?

Linda: That's right, although climate change will cause a certain shift. The large leaf of the lime tree will suffer from drought. You can already see this in hot summers, when the leaves roll up and only unroll again when it gets wet.

WW: The leaf's lovely heart shape is striking, and its jagged edge. Why does a heart-shaped leaf have these jags?

Linda: Our great heart is visible in the shape of the leaf it is true, but this does not mean that we relinquish ourselves entirely. We still retain our own character. You have to reckon with a few jagged edges, but they are discreet and friendly. The drop-like shape of the leaf shows our clear connection with fluidity, as can also be seen in our flowing nectar. Have you ever parked a car under a lime tree?

WW: I know the problem. Even the leaves are covered with a kind of resin or honeydew. What causes this?

Linda: We are very bountiful towards the insect world — we are an important summer tree not just for bees but also aphids.

Following the sumptuous blossoms in spring, the linden is the summer's chief provider of nourishment. Ants also milk the aphids on the leaves, sometimes even breed them, and ants are extremely important for loosening the soil.

WW: What relationship does the lime tree have with other trees?

Linda: The lime is an open-hearted and sociable companion to other trees. We have no problems with other trees, and they in turn like our company. The lime tree appears amidst all kinds of other trees, but equally is happy to stand on its own.

WW: What healing effect do lime blossoms have on people?

Linda: They protect against colds. If your body warmth drops, the lime blossom warms you again, and does so more strongly than elder. The elder possesses a more gentle warmth. Lime blossoms have an extremely warming effect and strongly combat infection. Lime blossoms also help people with severe fever, but unfortunately are difficult to dry.

WW: Planted on hills, lime trees visible from afar were once seen as trees of freedom. Why?

Linda: This is due to the tree's sacred quality. The lime tree was not just a tree embodying fertility, but anyone who found refuge in its protective crown could not be hung.

But fertility also has a direct connection with freedom. To put it in a nutshell, freedom can advance through the fact that people multiply. If they do not multiply, there will be no more people to grow into freedom. We are the tree of freedom, bountifulness and hospitality. This is why you find the name 'Linde' in so many place names and in the names of inns and taverns. People used to have a sense for this, and that's why they used my name so often.

The Caucasian Lime

Tilla x euchlora

WW: The Caucasian or Crimean lime tree was probably cross-bred from the small-leaved lime and another type of lime. What kind of tree is this?

Linda: It is not as bountiful as the large-leaved lime, and you can see this already in the shape of the leaves. It also tends to grow more in eastern regions — like the small-leaved lime — whereas the large-leaved lime is more of a western tree. I say 'more of' to avoid over-rigid interpretation. This means that in eastern regions bountifulness has to be grasped more through the I, the ego, than from one's surroundings. I am not thinking here of Chinese or Mongolian culture, but of Russia and the Balkans. In the East, bountifulness is not  mediated so strongly through trees. This is why the Caucasian lime also has somewhat smaller leaves and does not grow as tall as the large-leaved limes. The Caucasian lime is a tree bred by people.

WW: The leaves are obliquely heart-shaped and finely serrated, and have a shiny, dark green colour.

Linda: This shows that they cope better with dry conditions. This tree grows further from the Atlantic, in a more arid zone, whereas the large-leaved limes prefer humid, coastal climates.

Mass death of bumblebees

WW: At midsummer every year one can observe masses of bumblebees dying beneath silver and Caucasian limes. Why is this?

Linda: Sometimes bees and bumblebees only reach the limes when they have finished flowering. Instead of flying away they wait there, hoping for the nectar to start flowing. Some limes have already finished blossoming, others haven't begun. This too is a result of climate change, which makes the large-leaved linden tree flower ever earlier. When the bumblebees arrive too late, they starve beneath the limes.

WW: The dying bumblebees are not weak with age but in their prime; nevertheless they die under the limes, and what you say is very accurate. For a while people thought that the limes' nectar contained poison, but they experimented by feeding caged bumblebees exclusively with this nectar and found that none of them died. The reason, instead, is that the Caucasian and silver linden blossom two to four weeks after the large- and small-leaved linden. There is a 'nectar gap' in the intervening period. During this time the bumblebees get so weak that by the time the Caucasian and silver limes blossom, they are already too weak to feed. Climate change will probably extend this nectar gap.

Linda: Exactly.

WW: Why can't bumblebees lay up stores of nectar to survive this period?

Linda: Bees normally can do this; that's why they collect honey.

But people take more and more honey from them, thinking they will have enough supplies.

It's different with bumblebees that are not impaired by humans. The big question is: why doesn't the great bumble-being tell the bees under the lindens that there is no food there, and that they should fly away?

WW: Yes, that is certainly strange.

The start of personal destiny

Linda: This is also due to the fact that the Caucasian lime does not naturally grow in our latitudes, and has only been cultivated here recently. Bees and bumblebees are very future-oriented creatures and already, to a tiny extent, embody the human being's impetus of individuality. Bumblebees no longer listen to the great bumble-being because they are a touch similar to humans. Since ancient times the bumblebees have learned that a lime tree flowers in summer and that they can find nourishment from its nectar. But when other limes start growing here, they are not flexible enough to adapt; and since contact with the great bumble-being has also become more difficult, they are unable to alter their behaviour, and so starve to death.

Creatures are now undergoing developmental steps that correspond to a very early stage of humanity's evolution. Animals' individualization is increasing. This means that the influence from Devachan of the overarching creature, the animal ego, grows less strong on each individual animal, although the overarching creature does still send down certain impulses into each animal. When they begin — though still minimally — to develop a personal destiny, they make more mistakes.

But the main reason is that people plant other types of lime trees that the bumblebees here are not familiar with, and they find themselves locked out from a food supply.

WW: Could people help in some way?

Linda: They should finally recognize that they are the teachers of the animals. But in this case it's not easy, for humans can hardly collect the bumblebees together. Instead people should act as conscious exemplar to animals.

WW: But if you realize the kinds of displacement involved here, it should be possible to intervene. On the one hand you have bumblebees that are used to the nectar of the large-leaved lime. On the other the newly planted Caucasian limes. And between them the nectar gap. Surely we can use our conscious awareness to think through the problem, and thus give the great bumble-being new impulses that it can convey to individual bees. Couldn't the bumblebees learn new behaviour by this means?

Linda: Start doing it! That is a very good idea! It will work; there are enough examples of this from other realms. This is how it should happen. Convey your ideas to the great bumble-being. But if you humans do something like this, you must definitely make space for freedom. You must not send your thoughts to the great bumble-being in a way that compels it to do something. Above all you must teach the group-soul creatures freedom, or rather sensible ways of handling it. These beings certainly should not make all the same mistakes that you made — quite a few in fact!

All beings should talk to each other

WW: But I still find it strange that the connection between the great bumble-being and individual bumblebees does not work better, and that I as human being can conceive this communication disorder but am not easily able to remedy it.

Echevit, the Watery One: It's not strange. This shows that communication between people and nature spirits will be extremely important in future, and must continually be developed. This is what many of the nature spirits here in the mill keep emphasizing. Such disruptions of communication in nature can only be remedied if everyone talks to each other — that is, humans with nature spirits and vice versa. But this is an entirely new process. All need to speak more with each other:

nature spirits with humans, fire with water, the bumblebees with the linden etc. All beings must learn to express themselves and address one another. You humans have already learned to do this. If you examine your social fabric, you can see that problems between people arise when they do not speak to each other. To the extent that you demonstrate how to speak to each other, nature will take note of this and also learn it. The predominant role in teaching nature is passing to you humans, whether you desire it or not. If you Germans do not learn to speak with the Kurds and the Turks and others, bumblebees will not learn to talk with the lime trees.

WW: Nevertheless, I can't help objecting that people have developed freedom while animals and nature spirits have not. Currently, therefore, we can scarcely ask these other beings to grasp hold of a capacity that we humans are only now learning with great effort and difficulty.

Echevit: That is why it's good that you as human have the fundamental impetus not only to see this problem but also to resolve it.

WW: No, what I meant was that the great bumble-being would need to see this problem yet would also have to know at the same time that individual bumblebees are not free agents, and that it must therefore help them. Surely it should do so out of self-interest. I know this is putting it in human terms, but it also relates to the natural world.

Echevit: Of course; but nature too must in future learn to transmit things in a somewhat more individual way. The great bumble-being does not have a sense of the individual suffering of each bee, for the deaths of bumblebees under the lindens do not really threaten the whole species. Awareness that individual beings must be led in a more individual way must still arise. The great bumble-being will also have to learn this.

The Ash

Fraxinus excelsior

WW: Hello Lara. People recognize you in winter especially by your black buds. Can you tell me anything about your buds?

Lara: Hello. I am a sun tree. When the sun vanishes in winter, it is my night-time. When I bear leaves it is day for me and when I have no leaves it is night. The colour of night is black. It's really very simple.

The day angel

WW: Why is there such fine, felt-like down on these black buds?

Lara: I attract dew from the air with it. Dew is a very special fluid — you humans make too little use of it. Most people aren't even aware that such a thing exists. The morning dew contains what the bright face says. Do you know what this means?

WW: No.

Lara: Every morning, at the hour of dawn before the sun rises  over the horizon, but when it is already light, the day angel stands over the world. He passes once a day around the earth, you can say.

And at some point on his path he changes.

WW: Does he change daily with another angel?

Lara: Yes, every day the day angel, the bright face, is a different one. He can be perceived most clearly at dawn before the sun rises. This is the bright face, a special time of day. It's also the time when the morning dew falls. The angel imbues this dew with his particular quality. This is why spring days without dew, due to climate change, are so critical.

WW: Why?

Lara: Because the angel's blessing no longer reaches the earth. This down is something many trees possess, usually on their leaves. It is always there to absorb the day's blessing. I have them on my buds, too, not just on my leaves. It's because my buds can absorb this cosmic quality throughout the winter that I can form a special leaf.

Raining ash leaves

WW: What is the special quality of your leaf?

Lara: Since I am a sun tree I open my leaf entirely to the light.  Its real shape is the one that runs round all the leaflet tips. Everything that is open in me corresponds to the central vein of other leaves. The light being can enter into these openings. This in turn means that my leaf acquires a very special quality. The Romans planted the ash on their streets so that their animals could eat the leaves.

WW: I have also observed this in autumn: when the leaves of the ash suddenly fall, sheep rush to devour them.

Lara: Striking and typical of my species, and true only of a very few trees, is that when my leaves fall they all fall at the same time — you can say it rains ash leaves; and then my day is ending.

WW: And the leaves are green when they fall; they don't fade on the tree. Why?

Lara: They break off very smoothly at the ends of the stalks.

They are pushed away by the night, by the bud. They are still green when they fall because they have absorbed so much sunlight — and to give the animals a sun greeting in their autumn fodder.

Raising themselves through the power of Christ

WW: Is there anything more to be said about your leaves when they are hanging on the tree?

Lara: They turn with the sun and so take best advantage of the available light. Unlike many trees that protect their leaves from the sun's rays by turning their narrow edge to the sun, the ash leaf fully accompanies the sun so as to absorb all the sun power and quality. It does this the whole day. We ash trees can endure the full force of the sun; however we cannot stand in conditions that are too dry. We are not desert trees. We are strongly connected through the sun with the Christ being.

WW: Does this mean that during the day the tree acquires a left or right orientation at certain times?

Lara: Indeed. The ash is a tree of temperate zones and can therefore turn with the sun. With increasing aridity we will also suffer problems. If necessary we will shed our leaves.

WW: What significance does the ash have for human beings?

Lara: When the human being connects with the ash, he is always also in relationship with the Christ being. In our latitudes the ash is the tree that urges awareness of Christ.

WW: What significance does the ash have for nature and the nature beings?

Lara: If nature beings desire to connect with the power of the sun, they come to us ash trees. However not all beings do so, for instance the descending, degenerative powers do not. These beings mostly connect with the moon. Through its leaf quality, the fingers of the leaves, the ash conveys an outpouring of Christ power into the environment. Close to ash trees one can sense that various beings of the etheric world stream towards them, in order to raise themselves through the power of Christ.

WW: Is this then the significance of the ash tree for its surroundings?

Lara: Definitely.

Lording it like Caesar

WW: Does the ash have a special relationship with other deciduous trees?

Verena Staël von Holstein: Something is going on with the roots.

WW: Can you say anything about the roots of the ash in relation to other trees?

Lara: Other trees cannot use the roots of the ash and are hindered by them. The ash makes the soil unusable for other trees. If they enter the ash's domain, especially with their roots, they cannot endure it and die.

WW: Yes, this is true. It has been observed that stands of ash are often alone and other trees are suppressed. This is indeed connected with the main root of the ash. It grows vertically down for a short while but after a depth of about twenty centimetres it turns and grows horizontally. The ash also has very intense root growth. Beeches that grow alongside the ash have to delve their roots into ever deeper layers of the soil, which means that young beeches die in summer droughts. When little rain falls, the beeches can no longer meet their need for water since the ash trees drink it all first.

Lara: That's right. This is the other aspect of sun nature — lording it like Caesar, which is also a certain kind of solar quality: an exclusive claim to leadership. This Caesar quality undergoes change, however, and the ash's root does not wish to harm other trees close to it. Any tree whose root can grow down through the ash's root network will also find protection from the ash. The ash needs moist environments because it requires a lot of water. Ash trees are not forest trees and there are no real ash woods. The ash — usually planted by people — is often found along roads, and otherwise it stands in light-filled meadows, usually as a single tree.

WW: It has also been observed that ash trees in forests often grow very densely and numerously, but do not grow very tall and soon die. Why is this?

Lara: Because they need sunshine from all directions and follow the course of the sun with their leaves. If this is disturbed — for instance by the branches of other trees — and the ash can no longer follow the sunlight, it no longer wishes to live.

WW: The ash would in theory have to grow above the crowns of other trees in order to survive.

Lara: Yes, that's right. That's why ash trees do not usually grow in large numbers in forests. Because the ash follows the sun it can give back this sun quality through its leaf.

Ash leaves fortify sick animals

If a lot of ash leaves lie on the ground, are not eaten by astral creatures and start to rot, the soil can become unusable for other trees. The ash has to a small extent developed away from the etheric into the astral. This is due to its strong relationship with the rhythm of day and night.

WW: Are these astral aspects in the ash leaves also the reason why animals like eating them so much?

Lara: Yes.

WW: I have heard that in the Alps sick animals are still fed ash leaves.

Lara: Ash leaves strengthen their life forces.

WW: And why do the leaves decompose so quickly after falling?

Lara: They acidify the soil, and for other trees ash leaves have a somewhat astral, animal quality. Usually the problem is minimized by animals eating up the ash leaves; wild animals love ash leaves as much as domestic ones. They really graze the ash leaves, which means that the negative effect on the soil scarcely has an impact.

WW: Why does the ash especially like growing by flowing water?

Lara: Because flowing water is usually cleaner than standing pools. The ash's connection with the sun means that it requires its natural surroundings to be clean and pure. The ash does not cope very well with environmental pollution.

WW: What can you say about ash timber?

Lara: Ash is highly prized and used a great deal for making bows because of its elasticity. It's also durable, and so very high quality. You can make almost anything with it. Cradles made of sun wood are particularly good: an ash cradle endows a child with sun quality.

WW: Do the leaves and bark of the ash have a healing effect on human beings?

Lara: Some people stuff pillows with ash leaves for better sleep, but this effect is never very long-lasting. Once the leaf has dried it quickly disintegrates. But you can eat ash leaves as salad and will get strength from them just like the animals.

The ash as sacred sun tree

WW: Why was the ash regarded in the past as a sacred tree in northern Europe?

Lara: Because of its sun quality. Megalithic culture was strongly sun-oriented, partly because it had the task of observing how the sun being was gradually approaching the earth — how Christ was descending. This is also why people erected the great stone monuments, to observe events at Golgotha. And since the northern initiates possessed great clarity of awareness, they knew that the ash is the sun tree, and therefore gave it protection. This is also why ash mistletoe was regarded as a very special type of mistletoe. It played a special role in the healing arts of the Druids. However, mistletoe does not primarily grow on ash trees. It likes growing on poplars. Mistletoe is a young plant, and the poplar is also a young tree.

WW: In Anglo-Saxon regions there even used to be a death penalty for felling two ash trees.

Lara: That shows how important the ash was then. Stonehenge is an ancient sun observatory, and the Irish-Scottish monks also closely observed the Christ event at Golgotha. All of them were aware that the ash belongs to Christ.

Plunging sunlight into a vampire

WW: Is this why in vampire tales an ash stake is rammed into the vampire — because the ash has this sun quality?

Lara: That's right. In the night you plunge the sunlight into the vampire.

WW: There's an old saying that refers to the emergence of foliage in the spring: 'Oak before ash, in for a splash; ash before oak, in for a soak.' Does this still hold true today?

Lara: It's still relatively correct, although climate change means that all these old country sayings are less applicable. At the start of the year it's cold and wet, then comes the rainy period, and then high summer follows almost immediately. This means that the spring and summer processes are increasingly compressed: the springs become shorter and so the spring vegetation period is also shorter. Nevertheless the relationship between the two trees as the old rhyme puts it is true.

WW: Is there anything more you would like to say about yourself?

Lara: I wish that every human being would plant one ash tree in their life.

WW: Why?

Lara: To spread the Christ quality across the earth. When you plant trees, remember to note the tree's original compass orientation, so you can keep to the same orientation at the new growing site. This will suit the tree much better, and you will help it to thrive at its new location.

WW: Many thanks.

Lara: My pleasure.

Stonehenge

The European Beech

Fagus sylvatica

WW: Who would like to speak for the beech?

Verena Staël von Holstein: Letra, the beech being. This is not an individual beech.

WW: Hello Letra, a warm welcome.

Letra: Good day.

WW: What kind of tree is the European beech?

Letra: A tall tree, a very tall one. In contrast to many trees you have spoken with here, beech trees grow together in large quantities in woods and forests. There are great forests consisting only of beech, and the individual beeches feel very good in this community. The European beech — and this is logical for a forest tree — can cope with very little light. To begin with, when small, it grows very slowly; but when it receives more light it starts growing very fast. Because of this the beech can form large woods and forests. It forms very beautiful, long and straight trunks, which is why it's much in demand for forestry plantations. The beech is one of the best fuel woods, but its timber is also used for many other purposes, such as toy-making. In general, beech wood is very lovely, sometimes with magical markings. The beech is a typical deciduous tree of central European forests.

WW: And very adaptable?

Letra: Yes.

WW: One can even make hedges of the hornbeam beech.

Letra: Yes, but not of the common beech. Because of its trunk it has no capacity to grow low. For hedges you'd have to use the hornbeam, which closely resembles the beech, for instance in the shape of the leaves.

The conventional citizen

WW: What human quality does the beech correspond to?

Letra: An upright, average, law-abiding citizen. It also corresponds to someone who supports the state in a conventional way.

WW: But the beech leaves that appear at the beginning of May, with their very beautiful, fresh green vibrancy, don't really seem to fit with a conventional, stuffy quality.

Letra: Careful now, for many headstrong youths grow steady and conventional in middle age. It's often the case that young people who were once very bold and full of energy have the edges rubbed off them after a few years and then become cornerstones of society, whereas those who were compliant at the beginning later break out and go wild.

WW: What can you say about the shape of the beech leaf?

Letra: The beech has a very softly serrated leaf, and so no great defensiveness. In its shape you can say that it stands midway between all others: it is neither round nor angular, not long and jagged nor pinnate, but really very balanced in its proportions. The May green of the young leaves is of course the most

Young leaves and blossoms

beautiful. Scarcely any other tree has this typical May-time character.

Beechnuts

WW: Why do the blossom shoots appear at the same time as the foliage in spring?

Letra: Because it is practical to form both at once. The beech tries to flower at the same time as other surrounding trees in a forest so that a reasonable degree of pollination can occur. Later the beechnuts form in consequence. But this fruiting does not go equally well every year.

Nevertheless the beech has a very good connection with the weather beings. Its beechnuts orient themselves to the latter's requirements and each forthcoming winter period.

WW: So there weren't many beechnuts this year?

Letra: Relatively few. Though I have good contact with the weather beings I am not as flexible as they are, and climate change is causing me quite a few problems. I will have to gradually adapt because there will be fewer and fewer cold, snowy winters.

WW: Why are beechnuts usually triangular in shape?

Letra: The beechnut has a very unusual form. It's really formed in three planes standing in turn on a small, narrow surface. Beechnuts are pointed, longish and divided in three; they also taste excellent by the way. People can enjoy them too.

1 cm   1 inch

The self-development of the beech

WW: Why does the beech have a core of colour, which is often red, but often only appears after about eighty years?

Letra: The beech has a connection with the word 'book,' which is derived from it. In the old days people used to write on beech-wood boards because after they'd finished shrinking they lasted well. The red coloration of the wood comes from the beech's relationship to blood. The copper or purple beech is a particular beech cultivar, striking in its purplish leaves. Otherwise it's very similar to the common beech. The red colour always shows a connection with Mars. In its leaf shape the beech does not show any great defensiveness or antagonism; and only after a fairly long period of maturation does it come into some sense of itself. Before this the beech does not experience itself as an individual tree. Only at about the age of eighty does it start developing an identity, and demonstrates this with the red coloration.

When beech trees grow old they fall prey to severe, wood-eating fungi that start to dissolve the tree's tissue. Forestry has problems when there are many stocks of beech of the same age, because this kind of fungus can spread across wide areas. For this reason it makes good sense to cultivate beeches of different ages together.

Nowadays the beech still retains its main geographical spread and needs a relatively cool and balanced climate. If it grows too warm in our regions, the beech will have to give way to other trees. You can understand this if you look at its harmonious yet oval and very flat leaf, which shows that the beech leaf has a relatively high rate of evaporation. If longer periods of warmth or heat prevail, the tree will be weakened by losing too much moisture through its leaves. Other trees will then take up the spaces that become free.

WW: The leaves of the beech also grow very densely, even sometimes overlapping. Why?

Letra: Because the beech does not experience itself as an individual in its first decades, but as part of the whole forest. Only when it starts to sense a certain identity and forms the red core in its wood, does it reach a height where its crown is fully exposed to light. Before then it experiences itself as part of the surrounding wood, mixing amongst the various trees and also laying its leaves very modestly over each other.

WW: I have seen many beeches whose branches grow very haphazardly. Why is this?

Letra: Because they focus less on one tree. They don't really have a sense that their branches and twigs belong to the tree so much as to the whole wood. That's why beech twigs grow in all directions. A beech tree only starts forming itself when it is eighty.

WW: Is that why the beech plays such a subordinate role in folklore? As far as I know it doesn't figure there at all.

Letra: Yes, this is because the beech offers no definite perspective. It's there and is used: its wood was used for fuel, pigs were brought to graze on the beechmast — but the tree did not make a striking impact. That's why there are no special legends about it.

Water and lightning

WW: Is it true that beechwood cut at new moon lasts longer and is less susceptible to woodworm?

Letra: Yes, for the beech has a certain relationship with water. At new moon water is more contained and the tree is then more compact. That's why its wood is better then. At new moon more water leaves the tree.

WW: Does the beech have a special relationship with lightning?

Letra: There's an old saying relating to lightning: 'Cleave to the beech, keep far from the oak.' But please treat this with great caution, for the saying refers to the fact that the beech does not have a main taproot, since all beeches in a wood have a common root network. The oak on the other hand has a deep-delving taproot, which is why it can survive periods of drought, since the taproot goes down into the groundwater. People claim that the oak attracts lightning because of its contact with groundwater, and that likewise the beech does not attract it. Please remember, though, that a beech tree standing alone will draw lightning just as much as an oak standing alone. So you'd have to be very careful which beech you take shelter under. In storms it's best to go home and not stand under trees. This saying is not backed up by modern physics.

WW: Is there anything more to say about the European beech.

Letra: My wish would be for you to love the beech. And in my old age I am more individual than you imagine.

The Pendula or Weeping Beech

Fagus sylvatica forma pendula

WW: The pendula beech is related to the European beech and is also known as the 'weeping beech.' Why is this?

Letra: These trees are closely related. It's striking, however, that the leaf of the weeping beech is a good deal rounder. The weeping beech accentuates the watery element more strongly than the European beech, and its shape has a typically melancholic gesture. The shape of the weeping beech expresses lament or weeping.

WW: The form of the weeping beech is almost like a crystalline fountain.

Letra: Exactly. The weeping beech is the wettest beech. It is not nearly as common as the European beech and is more like a single tree: it manifests the melancholic type, as it were crystallizing this form out of water.

WW: Why don't weeping beeches grow any higher than twenty metres?

Letra: Because they are too melancholic. They gravitate too much towards the earth.

The Copper Beech

Fagus sylvatica forma purpurea

WW: We have already spoken of the red coloration and the relationship to Mars and iron. Can you say any more about this?

Letra: This tree is the individualist among the beeches. If you look carefully you can see a more jagged quality to the leaf edges than in any other type of beech. This is due to the Mars influence in the copper beech. Through this influence it develops a strong self-awareness at a young age. This Mars aspect comes right through into the serrations of the leaves.

WW: The leaves are also longer. Why is this?

Letra: They tend towards a lancet shape, thus expressing a much more defensive character. The copper beech also tends more to stand alone or in small groups, and does not form whole woods. You can regard a group of copper beech in a park as a small military unit, a little troupe of fighters on the defensive — the point of a spear that frees a passage for a large crowd behind. That's how you can see the copper beech.

WW: Why does the red or purplish colour fade towards autumn?

Letra: Because the more warring aspect of the copper beech

 diminishes as winter approaches. Seen in the context of a whole year, the copper beech becomes more peaceful towards autumn, for then it encounters Michael and no longer needs to be so combative.

WW: Why does the copper beech have such a smooth trunk, in contrast to the common beech?

Letra: The smooth quality protects the skin of the trunk from external influences. Smooth trunks signify that the tree is not open to its surroundings. Of all beeches the copper beech is the most individualistic. It is not as independent as the plane tree, but still very individual by beech standards.

The Hornbeam

Carpinus betulus

WW: Isn't the hornbeam also a very individual tree?

Letra: The most noticeable thing about the hornbeam is that its branches start spreading very soon. That's why it is good for hedge-laying and hedge-cutting. The hornbeam is a fairly knotty tree; it has a less smooth bark and a greater number of leaf-veins. The shape of the leaf is not quite so rounded and shows a marked orientation to the earth element. The attraction to rock means that it develops an almost indestructible solidity in its wood. This very tough wood is also noticeably grey, which points to stone-like qualities. It is often called stone or ironwood.

WW: Why do large animals like eating hornbeam twigs so much? Mice even eat the roots.

Letra: Because they want to absorb this tree's resilience. Animals are very fond of eating hornbeam foliage, although they like ash leaves still better. This foliage contains a great many minerals that the hornbeam absorbs through its very wide-reaching network of roots. It has few bitter substances, and

therefore tastes good. Oak leaves, on the other hand, are not popular with animals because of their high tannin content.

WW: What relationship does the hornbeam have with earthworms?

Letra: Since the hornbeam likes growing on walls or in hedgerows, or at the edge of fields, it has a special connection with small rodents and other small creatures. Earthworms multiply very happily in the hornbeam's root network. You find a good deal more earthworms there than in the roots of other trees. This is another indication of the hornbeam's strong preoccupation with soil processes, and this is also expressed in the almost rectangular leaf-shape. The

hornbeam is a tree with a great affinity for the soil. That's why it attracts beings that crawl through the earth, as soil turned to life — like the earthworms for instance. Where the hornbeam penetrates the soil, it enlivens it. This is why earthworms, which correspond to the earth's living element, are attracted by the hornbeam. Did you know that there are roughly 15,000 tons of earthworms in one square kilometre of forest?

WW: That many?

Letra: Yes indeed.

The Elm

Ulmus

The fluttering elm

WW: Hello Robert.

Robert: Good day.

WW: There are a great many different types of your tree: the field elm, the rock elm, the fluttering elm, the Huntington elm and many more. Why are there so many varieties?

Robert: Why are there so many different people?

WW: Well, there certainly aren't that many elms ...

Robert: You see, we are really very modest in our varieties! The elm embodies a principle that is expressed in the etheric; but in fact there are other types of tree that have produced considerably more varieties.

Generosity

WW: Which principle do you mean?

Robert: The elm's principle corresponds to generosity. This

is also why we have such an extreme reaction to human acquisitiveness. This is what triggers the death of elms. If this acquisitiveness continues to increase, ever more elms will die, for the generous human being will disappear likewise.

You can see this best from our leaf edges, for the two halves of each leaf start at slightly different points on the stalk. We give each half of the leaf its freedom.

On the other hand, the multiple serrations of the leaf edges have a somewhat outflowing character. In this outflow, though, a viscous quality is also indicated. It does not flow out so freely as the maple for example. In addition, any kind of profit-seeking harms us.

Elm wood is an old and very traditional furniture timber, which was used for making beds and good chests of drawers. The elm comes close to human habitations, and also grows in cities, but at the same time is a tree that can adapt to life in the forest. It does not have to adopt an individual position, but likes growing with other forest trees. This shows the elm's generosity. It does not have to stand alone.

WW: What relationship does the elm have to rivers and to water in general?

Robert: The elm needs a moist location and therefore grows best in flood plains. Without a river close by it does not feel good, because it cannot impart its generosity to anyone. That's why elms in particular are suffering from climate change if they grow in cities. Drought causes them real problems. The elm is a typical riverside tree and has a very close connection with rivers. It can also assume certain qualities from each river: the Elbe elm is somewhat different from the Oder elm.

WW: Why do very old elms have board-like extension fins that pass on into their roots?

Robert: Every older elm has this tendency.

These extensions form to give the trunk greater stability, as the tree does not make very extensive roots. When the elm grows tall above, it needs a counterbalance below, or else it would fall over easily.

WW: What can you tell me about the flutter elm's blossom clusters, which appear in loose bunches on the twigs before the foliage comes?

Robert: This also shows our generosity, for when we blossom we put forth great bunches of blossom. When we blossom we always make a whole image of ourselves. The blossoms of various elms correspond roughly to the shape of a tree: to our loose crown, which very generously allows light, air and everything else to permeate it.

WW: What can you tell me about the fruits that hang from the trees as broad-winged nutlets in loose seed-heads?

Robert: The fruits are nutlike and spread best through animal excrement after creatures eat these fruits.

Irregular

WW: The name 'elm' comes from the Latin Ulmus effusa, which roughly means 'irregularly dispersed.' This corresponds exactly to what you said about your permeable crown.

Robert: The spirits of creation endowed us with this irregularity. The leaf neck on both sides of the stalk is similarly irregular. Regularity stands in opposition to generosity. Unfortunately the elm's generosity gives rise to the problems we have already mentioned.

WW: In some ways the elm seems quite opposite to the beech. Do you agree?

Robert: Yes, you're right. Despite this, the elm — like the beech — appears in woods and forests, but embodies irregularity as a principle rather than in each individual tree.

WW: Why does the bark of all types of elm have long slits, and

 why does the bark of the flutter elm flake off in thin scales?

Robert: Because the bark is given away as a gift. Many creatures use the bits of bark for things such as nest building. Shedding bark also allows the elm to dispel toxins. Elmwood is a very beautiful wood, with a luminous red quality.

WW: Why is the flutter elm sensitive to early frosts but resistant to late frosts?

Robert: That's a slightly illogical way of putting it. Once the leaves reach a certain size they are no longer susceptible to frost, but they are still susceptible while they're emerging. Once the leaves have emerged into the world, the frost can no longer harm them. But before they've emerged fully, the frost can still do some harm. When the elm forms its leaves too early, they can be damaged by early frosts. It must therefore resist the temptation to form leaves prematurely, though this will become very difficult given the current climatic changes.

WW: Some people claim that the elm is sensitive to summer droughts, while others assert the opposite. Which is true?

Robert: This depends on the type of elm. An elm standing in flood meadows has very little sensitivity to summer drought since there will still be water available for a long time. If the elm is growing on a sandbank, it will be extremely sensitive to summer drought, for its roots do not go very deep. In a flood plain there is no need for deep roots. The different opinions of human beings are simply based on inadequate observation of elms.

WW: Is there anything more you would like to say about elms?

Robert: We have already discussed the theme of dying elms here.

I don't really have any more to say.

WW: Many thanks.

Robert: You're welcome.

Small robinia

The Black Locust or False Acacia

Robinia pseudoacacia

WW: Hello robinia. What is your name?

Clausine: My name is Klausine.

WW: With a K or a C?

Clausine: With a K. Don't you like the name?

WW: It would be lovelier and rounder with a C.

Clausine: Fine, I'm happy with that. But we robinias are not that rounded — only our leaves are somewhat rounded.

Everything about us is forked and loosened up to the light

WW: The black locust is a tree that grows up to thirty metres tall and has a round, light and airy crown. Large branches often fork off from the trunk close to the ground. Why does the locust grow in this way?

Clausine: We have a feathery gesture. We are an airy and light-filled tree and give ourselves up to the air element. To ensure that sylphs can penetrate us everywhere, we don't have

massive, gnarled branches. That's why everything about us is forked and loosened, which you can see primarily in our leaves. Everything is entirely devoted to the air. We are one of the airiest trees, and we love the sylphs.

WW: But your bark tends to be deeply furrowed and heavy. Why?

Clausine: A deep furrow also opens itself to the air. If you are entirely smooth you are completely sealed off. With deep furrows the air can penetrate you. It is usually very wet around Easter, and that's when most trees gradually acquire their leaves. We wait a little longer before our leaves come, because water is too heavy for us: we need light.

Our blossoms and fruit are also very airy. They are not large and heavy but fine and filigreed. The fruits hang down into the air element.

Thorns and heat

WW: Observing the leaves one sees a midrib with numerous oval leaflets. What else do these leaves express?

Clausine: The leaflets grow out from the main stem in pairs

relative to each other. Where the leaves join on to the tree there are two sharp thorns. Thorns are always formed when the fluid element is suppressed in favour of air and warmth. Plants that can endure great dryness tend to form thorns.

WW: Can you explain this a little more?

Clausine: Plants growing in hot places tend to form thorns because they do not work so closely with the undines. To put it figuratively, a sylph can sit upon a thorn tip, whereas an undine cannot. Thorniness is an expression of very strong etherization to the point of horn formation. If, as a tree, you give yourself to this etherization, you will develop leaves like ours. While they have a certain roundness they also have a filigree delicacy. Our leaf is not heavy, and our actual leaf shape can be perceived in the outer circumference of the whole leaf. This longish shape is further opened by the separate leaflets, so that light and air can penetrate everywhere.

Despite this, we live in harmony with the undines and also lead them towards the light. We have no problems with the drop form: our part-leaflets are long and round and thus show their affinity with water. Really this corresponds to the droplike and watery, to the dewlike.

WW: Why do your leaves have no serrations or jags?

Clausine: Because you should see the leaf-tips themselves as jags. We don't wish to injure the air and therefore we have thorns only below on the leaf stalk. Apart from our thorns we are a very gentle plant.

Sweetness and readiness for love

WW: Your white blossoms are striking, often hanging in clusters ten to fifteen centimetres in length, with a strong, fragrant

smell. What can be said about this scent and the blossoms?

Clausine: The locust not only loves the air but also everything that lives in it: the insects that fly through the air. It attracts these insects with its strongly

perfumed flowers.

The bee is a sun being. As well as its warmth the sun also has a light quality. God's might is revealed in the light. Our blossoms try to attract everything that exists in light and airy spaces. With their sweet scent our blossoms symbolize love; wherever sweetness arises in the plant kingdom, there is always a readiness for love, and at the same time also the longing to make contact with other beings. We open ourselves wide to the small beings of the air. You can eat our blossoms, but the rest of us is fairly poisonous.

Poison

WW: Why is the black locust so poisonous? If you eat only four seeds, nausea, vomiting and diarrhoea will strike after an hour.

Clausine: This is because our seeds are permeated with a strong astrality, due to our dedication to the light and air. The next higher level can therefore enter us better. Wherever the astral enters the plant kingdom, strong poisons develop. The astral has a strong light quality, which you can also find in starlight.

WW: Even when working your wood, one can be poisoned by breathing in the sawdust. Why does a tree as beautiful as you at the same time have such an antagonistic character, expressed in poison and thorns?

Clausine: You experience beauty on the one hand, and poison and thorns on the other as contradictory. We don't experience it like this. The thorns have a gesture similar to poison: an astralization of the etheric space occurs in them.

Because we are closely related to the air element, we can grow well on poor, sandy soil and don't have to live in marshy conditions like the willow. That is why we have a certain  animal-like character. The animal has a gesture of dedication to the human being, informing the whole feeling realm of people in the physical world. In every animal, at least, one can perceive a certain archetypal human emotion, a one-sided aspect. When a tree — as the highest plant being, and closest to the animal realm — extends into the astral sphere, you get beauty and lightness on the one hand, but on the other a pronounced toxicity, because we are already animal-like. This is not a contradiction, but an inevitable necessity.

WW: But one thing still surprises me: deadly nightshades are poisonous for humans but not for animals. Why is the locust particularly poisonous for animals, primarily for horses, and also dogs, rabbits and birds?

Verena Staël von Holstein: It is hard to understand what she is saying. Could you repeat that Clausine?

Clausine: In the deadly nightshade family the proximity to the animal is not as pronounced as in me. The stronger this is, the more poisonous one becomes for all ensouled creatures. Black locust wood helps, for instance, to keep beetles away from a house, as they don't like crawling over it. The wood also helps against other so-called pests, for instance mice.

Horses die from the poison

WW: Reports from the First World War recorded that 32 horses out of 120 died in one night after nibbling robinia wood. The first animals died after only four hours. Why?

Clausine: Horses have very sensitive stomachs. You need much more poison to kill a chicken than a horse. Horses also have a very sensitive digestive system and die relatively easily from toxins. Although they look very powerful, they can quickly die if their digestive system is affected.

WW: Your fruits make long, twisting pods that grow up to eleven centimetres in length. Why do you form fruit in this way?

Clausine: The shape of the pods is so they can fly well. While they are relatively compact, they have an affinity with the light and air. They turn easily and flutter a little. However, we don't multiply as easily as the birch. We find transplantation somewhat difficult.

WW: Is it true that in homeopathy a remedy can be made from the locust for stomach acidity and migraine?

Clausine: Yes, certainly. The false acacia is a classic remedy. The homeopath Hahnemann worked very specifically with poisons. He diluted them and assumed — and he was right — that potentized toxins cure what in normal concentrations would poison. As potentized remedy, therefore, I cure what would happen if you eat me in a pure state. In the latter case you would have severe stomach problems. And in the human being the stomach and head are connected.

WW: What kind of relationship do you have with other trees?

Clausine: Relatively neutral. There are no tree communities with which I fit particularly well. It's not like the birch and pine which often grow together and are very happy next to one another. I get on very well with bushes and there is something bush-like in the gesture of my own twigs. Since I grow fairly tall, and bushes grow beneath me, I live harmoniously with them. All other pinnate trees, too, such as the rowan, get on well with me. My poison does not affect plants. In Europe I appear in the wild, but can also be found in parks there.

Cynicism

WW: Is there a human quality that corresponds to you as tree?

Clausine: This is connected with cynicism in a certain sense — very clear thinking on the one hand, and poisonous on the other. Whoever wishes to cultivate a healthy cynicism should sit for a while under a robinia. I embody clear penetration of the environment with thought, connected with the greatest bitterness and toxicity.

Excess acidity

WW: Why isn't it good for locusts to grow close to stretches of water?

V Staël von Holstein: Now she seems lost for words. Echevit, why isn't this good?

Echevit: It is not bad for the water but for the creatures living in it. If robinia leaves and other parts of the tree fall in the water, creatures living there can be poisoned. This is why, for instance, people with fishing lakes don't let black locusts grow by the water's edge. The tree itself has no problem by the water. They can over-acidify it, though, because they nitrogenize the soil, which is then washed into the water. Nitrogenization of water also leads to a massive growth of algae. Something similar occurs through fertilizer run-off: rivers are over-fertilized and then riotous growth takes place, covering the surface. In summer you can have a whole pond or other standing water covered in dense water lilies. But in fact the nitrogenization caused by robinias is substantially less than run-off caused by humans. That needs to be weighed in the balance.

WW: Is there anything more you wish to say?

Clausine: I would like you to take pleasure in my airiness and give yourselves more fully to the light — but in doing so try not to become poisonous.

WW: Many thanks.

Clausine: You're welcome.

The Honey Locust

Gleditsia triacanthos

WW: Close to where I live, right in the middle of town, stand two honey locust trees, although they don't come from our latitudes at all. In fact they come from eastern North America and grow up to fifty metres tall. They are very slender below and become ever broader above. What kind of trees are these?

Ina: Hello Wolfgang. I am the tree in front of your door, where it is actually a little dry for me. You could water me now and then. We came here from North America and feel a little out of place in this region. We look rather similar to the black locusts but in fact we are quite different in nature. Our leaflets are not paired, and the shape of the leaf is also markedly different, con-verging in a point. The leaflets are  considerably smaller than those of the robinia. It is true that I am poisonous, but not nearly so much as the black locust. The honey locust's leaves are supremely fine and delicate. We are more lace-like than the robinia. Our fruits, also, are much larger.

Community forming

WW: These fruits are very interesting. The honey locust pods are indeed much bigger than those of the black locust, growing up to fifty centimetres in length. In autumn they twist and go brown. Why does the tree form fruits like this?

Ina: We are curved because the pressure towards excess is contained in the whole form of this pod. This is a principle inherent in the American continent. When our fruits fall down and open, the lentil-like seeds are eaten by animals. Birds can digest them, though they are hard to prise from their leathery capsules. This is easy for people but not for animals: the seeds' enclosure is a protective gesture. Many seeds are contained in each leathery pouch instead of a single seed

which, in the case of most other trees, finds its way independently into the world. This community of seeds in the pod expresses a group impetus, and you will also discover this in my leaf. If you look at the whole leaf as single entity, you can find the group within it. A light-oriented group is formed in my leaves. As a tree I have the marked tendency to form a community.

WW: What does it mean that such a light and airy tree, with so many filigree leaves, forms such a tough, leathery pouch as fruit?

Ina: The leathery pod forms a protective cloak around the group of seeds, and to a small extent there is a tribal sense at work here. This leathery fruit forms a tribal awareness with the seeds that lie within it, a group consciousness. This impetus is clearly discernible in us, and naturally we wish to pass this on to the creatures that live on us.

Crown of thorns

WW: Why do you have irregular and randomly grouped thorns on your twigs and branches?

Ina: These long, sharp thorns have given us the appellation 'Christ Thorn' because our long, sharp thorns recall the crown of thorns placed on Christ's head by Roman soldiers on the way to the crucifixion. The thorns are primarily located on the trunk and branches, and indicate defensiveness against creatures that wish to climb the tree — for we wish to protect our community in the crown. The fact that these thorns are found in very irregular and sporadic positions on the trunk indicates our airy quality. If the trunk bristled with thorns all over, a different element would be at work.

In passing I'll mention — since we know each other well and see one another almost every day — that you could also arrange your tree book according to the different elements to which trees are assigned: trees corresponding to the earth,

 water and air elements, and fire. But the latter type are rarer. It is clear that I belong to the airy trees, while the oak does not.

WW: What does the oak belong to?

Ina: It belongs to the water or earth trees. The oak is assigned to Mars, and is thus also watery.

WW: The leaflets of the black locust appear in pairs along the stalk, whereas yours do not. What is the significance of this difference?

Ina: A certain chaotic element comes to expression in us, as can be seen in our irregular thorns. Where leaves appear in pairs, the tree's organizing principle is stronger. If the leaves are not paired, there is greater chaos penetrating all the tree's processes. That is the main difference.

Soul affinity

WW: Does any human quality correspond to you?

Ina: Forming groups of thoughts; soul affinity and thus experiencing oneself as a group. I am the tree of soul affinity.

WW: Are you thinking here of people who strive for a higher, soul-spiritual community?

Ina: Yes, such efforts are supported by my nature. At the same time I also embody the tendency to protect such communities.

WW: Do you mean a certain fortress mentality?

Ina: Precisely.

WW: Many thanks.

Ina: You're welcome

Birch

The Silver or Weeping Birch

Betula pendula

WW: Now I'd like to take the birch tree.

Verena Staël von Holstein: As a child I had my first encounter with nature spirits amongst birch trees.

WW: What exactly did you see?

V Staël von Holstein: The birch beings who I played with. I talked to them in a dreamy way and kept coming back to visit them.

WW: What did they look like?

V Staël von Holstein: Like young girls. The birch has a very maidenly character.

WW: Is there a birch that can speak with us?

V Staël von Holstein: Of course there is, and her name will scarcely surprise you: she is called Birka.

Rejuvenating

WW: Hello Birka. Can you tell us something about yourself?

Birka: Hello. You have just been talking about my nature. I embody all that is childlike and maidenly in a wide range of different birch trees. No one would consider an oak maiden-like, but even a very tall birch still retains a graceful, slender quality, something vital and dedicated to the sun. You know the lovely old legend, do you, in which trees follow after the sun?

WW: Yes.

Birka: The birches are the last to still do this. The underlying principle of our being is embodied in all that is young, cleansing, rejuvenating. Birch tea expels water, makes people lighter and more youthful, relieves them of heaviness, washes toxins out of them. Birch elixirs make the skin more youthful. Among trees we embody feminine youthfulness above all.

WW: The birch seems to thrive in quite a range of different soils, particularly very poor ones. Where does the birch get this capacity?

Birka: It is because we are so young and have so much life force. The soil is of minor importance due to our youthful qualities. If we get enough water with the rainfall, we can even grow on scree. We simply have a great deal of life energy.

WW: Birch roots can grow both vertically and on the surface. Why can the birch do this?

Birka: We really only need water. We are survival artists. Do you remember when you were young and could manage with just a little sleep and food, and still had energy? That's what we are like. We are youth itself. We cope with more or less anything.

Hope for the coming spring

WW: The birch's lithe branches respond to the slightest breeze, giving the tree a very flexible, supple character. What is expressed by this flexibility and movement?

Birka: The sunny nature of youth. The bright green of our foliage also expresses this youthfulness, although our leaves can turn

a dark green or dusty colour. What we do find hard to bear is lack of water. If the summer is too dry some of our leaves turn golden and we cast them off. We do this to spare our strength.

Our catkins also show us to be a tree of youth. If a strong blast of wind buffets a birch tree, you can see our seeds flying everywhere. This tendency, to give away everything, is also due to our youthfulness. If the weather gets bad and winter comes, we close ourselves up, simply shut down until the next spring. Our hope of the coming spring lies deep in our being.

WW: Is this the human quality that corresponds with you?

Birka: Yes. You will never lose hope if you keep a birch branch in your house.

WW: What relationship does the birch have to light?

Birka: A very strong one, though primarily to morning light, less to midday light.

WW: Why morning light especially?

Birka: Because there is something very youthful about the morning. In midday light we can sometimes look a little grey and withdrawn.

Innocence

WW: Why is birch bark so white?

Birka: Because it expresses innocence, quite simply! And our bark is watertight — not just largely but entirely. That too is an innocent principle.

WW: Sealed off against external influences?

Birka: Yes, sealed and unassailable. Innocence can also be a very great protection. We are not attracted to dirt.

WW: What can you say about the leaves of the silver birch, which are pointed at the tip, even if not so sharply as the grey birch?

Birka: The grey birch does not grow here, and is the American version of us. Our leaf movement is very dynamic, though not as much as the poplar. The leaves have a heart shape as an indication of our very friendly nature. We are also very willing to help, growing first on a soil to prepare it for other trees to take root there. The leaves have a clear vein, which shows that we can handle dryness relatively well. Our leaves are also tougher and less soft than those of the lime tree. The serrations on the leaf-edge show our openness to light and air, but at the same time also a certain capacity to defend ourselves. This is the same principle as our innocence and the almost impenetrable bark.

Serrations and warmth orientation

WW: I'd like to ask a rather general question: we spoke about thorns with the black and honey locusts, and the fact that a tree with thorns has an affinity with warmth. Is it the case that a leaf whose edge is serrated has an affinity with light and warmth?

Birka: The exception proves the rule. The fine indentations tend in this direction, but take a look at an oak leaf for a moment. It is rounded but also has a notched edge. This means that the oak leaf also tends towards warmth. Wherever a notch or indentation appears there is a tendency to pass into warmth or rather to absorb warmth into the self. Serrations are also where the astral manifests a little. However in us the astral element is not strongly pronounced.

The birch is very healthy for people. You can even eat our leaves, although they are rather bitter. We are not poisonous at any rate. In bitterness you find the beginning of an astrally grown material. We are merely bitter, not toxic.

Allergies

WW: Why are so many people allergic to birch pollen?

Birka: This is usually a general allergy to pollen, and trees have a great deal of pollen. Human allergies have very little to do with our tree nature, but with the condition increasingly affecting humans: they are suffering boundary problems since their etheric body can no longer maintain itself against all that bombards their senses. This is what causes rising numbers of allergies. It has little to do with us trees and other pollen-producing beings, but more with changes in humans and their developing awareness of their etheric bodies. Not all humans are becoming clairvoyant to the same degree; but this change in their constitution is giving rise to severe allergies.

WW: Why do birches grow so fast, and why don't they live to be older than a hundred?

Birka: Have you ever seen a young person over a hundred?

WW: Hardly.

Birka: Then you have answered both questions together.

WW: So you always wish to retain your youthful nature, and therefore grow fast and do not grow very old.

Birka: Exactly. At a certain point we start to decay. Close by here stands a big sister of mine who is already approaching her end, and is too old now for a birch.

WW: How can the birch survive the most severe frost?

Birka: Why does an adolescent not get cold? Because he is in movement, has inner warmth, and because the fire beings are very active in him, stimulating the sex organs to become mature and so on. It is similar with the birch, although — to put it metaphorically — they also often catch cold. But they have no inner experience of doing so. We also have very strong fertility because birch seeds are extremely vital. Wherever they fall we grow and germinate. This pronounced fertility is one of our qualities. Likewise we have a great deal of salamander quality — that is, warmth — which is why we don't feel the cold.

The light of the North

WW: Do you have a special relationship with northern latitudes —
  with the landscape there and its people?

Birka: Of course. The further north you go, the more the landscape's
  light qualities are enhanced, as can be seen from the change
  between polar night and polar day in the summer. Have you ever
  visited a northern land in summer and seen the intense light
  prevailing there? There is something of this quality in Flensburg.
  That's why the birch is not a tree of the tropics, as there is too
  little light there. We need the light of a northern landscape, and
  along with it also the gnomes and other beings flitting around.
  Trolls don't like us though.

WW: Why?

Birka: Because birch trees root in the stone and rock where trolls
  have their troll cairns. In the North, in fact, where trolls live,
  increasing numbers of troll cairns are appearing. Humans also
  keep building such cairns, sometimes without any reason.

WW: Do you have any more to tell us?

Birka: Be young! I am the tree of headstrong, crazy youth.

WW: OK, but maybe without the crazy bit.

Birka: Good.

WW: Many thanks.

Birka: You're welcome.

Troll cairn on Trollstigen

Willow

The White Willow

Salix alba

WW: Hello Cara. Do you speak for all willows?
Cara: Hello Wolfgang. Yes I do.

Fiery and watery

WW: The silver willow is really the biggest willow that grows in our latitudes. Why does it have such a loose and open crown?

Cara: The crown is so open because the willow embodies a connection between the fiery and watery elements. It can form isolated branches which themselves are almost like a single tree. This is also one of the reasons why the crown is so loose. The white willow is indeed the type that grows tallest; it can develop into a massive tree. On the other hand you often see it in a bush-like form. This depends on the surroundings where it grows. The wetter its location, the thinner its trunk. This is quite logical since a thick trunk cannot grow on very wet soil.

WW: What can you tell me about the shape

of the leaf, in particular the longish leaves with white down on the underside?

Cara: These leaves are shaped like an icicle, and represent the principle of sluggish yet still flowing water: a kind of 'thick' water. At the same time they are informed by a radiant quality and are like a sort of rain shower or a garden fountain sprinkling earthwards — radiant water.

The leaves of the various different willows are very hard to distinguish from each other. The underside of my leaves has a noticeable silvery sheen. My leaves are also fairly fluid in movement, and when a breeze blows I can look almost white.

Weeping willow

On such occasions you can also detect my relationship with the moon. Moon and water are closely connected.

WW: What can you tell me about your wood?

Cara: My wood has a reddish-brown or reddy-orange core, which reveals the other aspect of my nature: that is, my connection with the element of fire. This element also manifests in leaf serrations. Although the white willow itself does not have such serrations, other types of willow do. Round-leaved willows, which also exist, have a fine serration in their leaves.

WW: The leaves of the weeping willow are also finely serrated, and are longer and more pointed than yours.

Cara: That's right.

Ghosts in hollow trunks

The willow can grow very old, and its trunk may lean or fall and become gnarled and knobbly. Such willows tend to form hollow trunks and, as people should grow increasingly aware, these cavities fill with beings. In my case these are mainly ghosts.

WW: What are ghosts really?

Cara: Ghosts arise from human beings who were too strongly connected with their earthly existence. There are a great many ghosts around today.

WW: What do the ghosts say to you, or what do you say to them?

Cara: The ghosts lament and desperately try to loosen their connection with material existence. We tell them to be patient. Very roughly, 200 years is the average time a ghost spends on earth. We try to explain to them that they should connect themselves with the etheric Christ if they wish to release themselves from matter. Then, in the afterlife, they can try to learn how to pray. But this is much harder to do then than when they are still embodied.

WW: Is it possible at all?

Cara: Only tentatively. If they prayed as children they may be able to recall this and start to pray again. But people who never learned to pray during their lifetime find this extremely difficult in the afterlife.

Salix alba 'Tristis'

Death and mourning

WW: Why were willows formerly regarded as trees of infertility and dishonour, of mourning and grief?

Cara: For people who lived in the sentient soul (that is, in their immediate sense impressions), the gesture of the willow gave rise to a sense of grief, which used to be commonly associated with death. For instance they would grieve for the loss of relatives, as in those days people felt very closely connected to other family members and did not live as isolated as they do today. The gesture of willows offered an image of grief and mourning. The image of the weeping willow immediately entered the human sentient soul, and so it was linked with death.

Many willows grow on heathland or moor, and people found this combination of moor and willow as not belonging to this world. The connection with infertility derives from the fact

Crack willow

that willows are not sown, although the gesture of the willow catkins is seed-spraying dissemination. Instead they were propagated vegetatively by planting a willow shoot, which took root and grew. In former times this was regarded as unfruitful propagation: not through seeds but through scions.

We are also enormously flexible, as a quality of solidified water. This assumes an almost crystalline form in the crack willow. If you break off a crack willow leaf it is like fracturing or cracking something.

Alleviating pain

WW: What is the willow's significance for medicine?

Cara: The bark expresses our fiery character. It contains salicylic acid, which is an old remedy for fever and pain. The substance brings on a fever if it won't come, and lowers a high temperature. Willow bark can even soothe severe pain, although salicylic acid is hard on the stomach.

WW: How does this salicylic acid content alleviate pain?

Cara: The remedy is in the form of grated and dried willow bark, made into a powder. Pain is like an inflamed surface, and by sprinkling the powder over it, you can't see the pain any more: it is covered over. In medical terms the pain is numbed. The acetylsalicylic acid blocks the pain receptors as if a thin layer of powder were strewn over them. This medicine has long been known, and it was one reason why the spirits of creation formed the willow in this way.

It also serves to enliven the areas on which it grows. The willow has problems today, however, since it is no longer used so much and therefore gets too woody. People sometimes fail to cut back willows from a false notion of environmental preservation. If they are cut back, willows renew themselves. Then they don't get so woody and hollow, and so fewer ghosts take up residence in them.

The heads of basket willows have something of a human form, and in the past people cut willow shoots to weave baskets from them. This is scarcely the case any more.

WW: Should we block the holes in willows, or leave them in peace?

Cara: There are more important holes to block first. The holes that arise from excessive exploitation of resources are far greater, so a couple of little holes in old willows are insignificant in comparison. And at least the ghosts have a place to live.

Wakeful intelligence

WW: What other qualities do you have?

Cara: Unlike birch I am a very intelligent tree. Because it keeps forming shoots and saplings, a willow is usually a great deal older than you might think, but still the same tree. This means the willow is awake and intelligent. It is one of the most wide-awake trees of all.

WW: Is the willow not necessarily well-disposed towards human beings?

Cara: Yes and no. We know people very well, and also, specifically, their inconsiderate ways with nature.

WW: How would you describe the human soul quality that corresponds to you?

Cara: Overcoming, for instance of the ghost state; the overcoming of illnesses and pain, and of rigid forms; the overcoming of dishonourableness, or of any pathological condition.

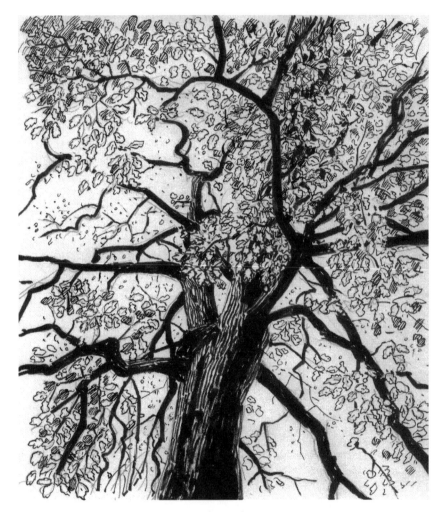

The oak

The English or Common Oak

Quercus robur

WW: Hello Oakbeen.

Oakbeen: Hello Wolfgang.

WW: There are many different types of oak. The English or common oak is one of the most widespread in our latitudes and figures strongly in the awareness of people living here. Why is this?

Oakbeen: That's very simple: it's because oaks used to be sacred trees and were dedicated to Odin. They figured in human minds as the most important trees of all. Have you ever seen a proper terp or dwelling mound?

WW: Yes.

Oakbeen: Do you know why people so often planted oaks on them?

WW: As protection probably.

Oakbeen: But against what?

WW: I don't know.

Oakbeen: You are ignorant. They were to protect against ice: ice-breaker oaks. Along the Elbe river, for instance, there were many ice-breaker oaks. When the Elbe flooded and the floodwater turned to ice, the oaks broke it up. An oak is an extremely solid, stable tree.

Endurance and stability

WW: Is the essence of the oak therefore endurance, or something else?

Oakbeen: Oh, a great deal more. The oak has the problem that its overseeing planet, Mars, has changed in significance, as has the metal assigned to it, iron. The wood of the oak is very hard, and when immersed in water even more so: it can survive centuries or even millennia.

Mars has generally been assigned a connection with warfare and was the Roman god of war. The Greeks called him Ares, and in Teutonic myth he was called Tyr. The corresponding day is Tuesday. However, the god to whom the oak was assigned in northern and central Europe is Wotan or Odin, who has a quite different quality from Mars. If you ponder this at leisure you can sense that the Teutonic peoples had an inkling of this change in meaning. Gautama Buddha went to dwell on Mars, a process which did not just happen from one day to the next. But Buddha transformed Mars into a planet of love. Buddha changed Mars from an iron-hard planet of battle to a leading planet of loving kindness. This was a Christ-like event.

WW: Let us return to you as tree: the common oak forms a lanky and widespread crown. What can you tell us about this shape?

Oakbeen: Since I am an expansive and lanky tree, I need a corresponding crown. You can find shade beneath this crown. You can also find protection there, given by the chief of the Nordic gods. I would like to point out, however, that other siblings of mine amongst the oaks have very different crowns — although almost all of their crowns are large. Oak trunks can be very different from each other: some put on thick girth immediately while others have very tall trunks. We tend to have a broad girth, and here you can see our power of endurance and durability.

WW: What can you tell me about the bark of the oak? In youth this is smooth and a brownish colour or even a whiteish grey, whereas in old age it becomes extremely thick with vertical fissures.

Oakbeen: Oak bark contains a tanning agent and has a very high tannic acid content, which enhances digestion. In former times people used oak bark for removing fur from animal skins and tanning them. Oak bark has an astringent effect.

The individualist among trees

Furthermore we have a pronounced individuality. Every oak has its own character — a different one for each tree I mean. As a human being when you encounter such a tree it is like  the meeting of two selves. This individualism usually penetrates right into the separate acorns. An acorn is very hard and compact — has one ever fallen on your head? It hurts and will certainly make an impact on you. With a birch or willow, on the other hand, it wouldn't.

WW: Why does the oak form such a deep and powerful taproot?

Oakbeen: Its depth means I can survive well in relatively dry conditions. Some oaks can even grow in desert regions. The convex bulges on my leaves also show that I cope well with heat. The leaves of the common oak are rounded and at the same time have a leathery quality, so I evaporate less water through my leaves than softer leaves do.

WW: Why are both the crown and the leaves so irregular?

Oakbeen: Every leaf of mine also has something individual about it. We are, quite simply, the tree of individuality, an impetus that's also connected with iron and meteoric iron.

WW: Why do the leaves have such short stalks?

Oakbeen: This is not true of every type of oak, but it is of the common oak. Its acorns sit singly on a stalk, whereas you may get two or three together on other oaks. The leaf stalk is what gave me my German name, Stieleiche or stalk-oak. But actually it has scarcely any stalk at all. The sessile oak has a longer leafstalk, but we are not that different in character.

Lightning conductor

WW: Why do oaks often divide into numerous branches quite near the ground, giving the impression of two trees, or rather a two-tiered tree?

Oakbeen: This is often the result of a lightning strike. Since we have a connection with iron, as lightning does, the oak is very often struck by lightning, more than any other tree. It is mere supposition that the taproot is responsible for this. The crown often divides at the scar where the lightning struck.

There's another reason for this split, too, which lies in our protective nature. You can protect a greater area if you divide up above. Oaks with a long, straight trunk usually have a less expansive crown than those which divide very early on. This division of the trunk and crown allows us to include a greater area under our protection. In northern Germany, it was common to cultivate oak copses because they provided pig fodder, were seen as trees of Odin and served as protective trees. They also acted as local lightning conductors. The oak offers not only spiritual but also physical protection.

Closing wounds and healing

WW: Can you expand a little on my earlier question about the bark?

Oakbeen: Our bark has a distinctive quality. If you saw off an oak branch, the wound seals up again. A wound can seal entirely, which is one reason why we grow so old. If our wounds are not too severe we can always close them up, and this is a property that has medical uses. We help close up and heal wounds in 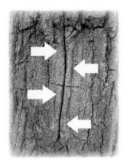 human skin. One result of this characteristic, however, is that the oak loses its smoothness with increasing age, since our bark interacts intensely with the air and becomes fissured. The oak's warmth emerges in the same way that the crust of a loaf opens during baking; but this is also the area in which the oak can heal.

We cast off our acorns

WW: What can you tell me about the shape of acorns and the cups in which they sit?

Oakbeen: There are cups of varying sizes: some come almost halfway up the acorn while others are so shallow that the acorn can scarcely sit in them. The formation of this part is again an expression of our strong individualism. You can almost say that the acorn is sitting on a presentation dish and can easily be released from the tree. We are the complete opposite of the honey locust and its leathery fruits: we release our fruits whereas they keep them for themselves. We cast off our acorns and give them away. That is our gesture. In former times, as I mentioned, pigs were herded into oak woods and the ones which ate us gave the best bacon.

The shape of the acorn also embodies the oak's tendency to be itself. It does not hide away but shows the world that it is a courageous tree. You won't get off very lightly if you try to pick a fight with me!

Sometimes we have branches in our crown without foliage: in other words, we carry dead wood around with us. When these branches and twigs are cast off during the next strong wind, we can easily heal the wounds they leave. We are vulnerable but can heal up again.

WW: Why do the oak's leaves stay hanging on the tree right into winter?

Oakbeen: Our leaves are not really dispelled by frost but instead pushed away by the new buds. Depending on the temperature, these buds form either in the autumn or in spring. We have a relationship with warmth. When warmth fades we keep our old leaves as a protective coat.

WW: Why is your wood such high quality?

Oakbeen: Because it's so dense. It is hard, easily split, and also often shrinks. But if well-stored it is extremely dense. The timber is reddish-brown in colour, which visually emanates a great deal of warmth.

WW: Please reflect on the human being and tell me which quality in him corresponds to you.

Oakbeen: Down-to-earth straightforwardness, positive fatherly qualities but not in a despotic sense. We also correspond to the human protective instinct, along with a fighting spirit and endurance.

WW: What is the gall wasp's relationship to the oak?

Oakbeen: That's really very simple. The oak has a bitter quality, a

Common oak gall wasp

very high tannin content. This is why it needs a creature that can cope with this extreme bitterness to fertilize it. This is why the spirits of creation made the gall wasp. The gall wasp lives with the oak: it cannot survive without us, and we need it for fertilization. The gall wasp lives in symbiosis with us. You humans have also made use of the gall wasp; you used to prepare ink from its cocoon. You no longer need to do that.

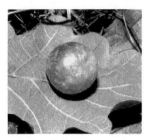

*Gall of the common
oak gall wasp*

This corresponds with Odin, who hung for four days on a windy tree and was wounded because he brought writing into the world. The first runes were etched in wood with stone, and later on people began to use ink.

The Red Oak

Quercus rubra

WW: The leaves of the red oak have a quite different character from those of the common oak. Besides being larger, their lobes are very pointed at the tip. Why is this?

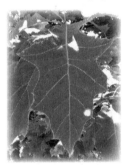

Oakbeen: The red oak originally comes from Canada or northern USA. You can see the rounded quality only in the inside indentation of the leaf because it has various sharp tips on the outside. This shows a different way of relating to etheric forces. The red oak has a somewhat aggressive engagement with forces of warmth: instead of a more watery quality it has a sharp and fiery aspect. In North America this type of oak tends to grow together in stands, and its leaves have much more pronounced veining and sharpness.

Slaughter

WW: Why do the red oak's leaves turn red in the autumn, while those of the common oak do not?

Oakbeen: Because too many thoughts of blood were around as this tree was developing.

WW: How do you mean?

Oakbeen: It's rather unpleasant. Do you really want to know?

WW: Certainly!

Oakbeen: It is connected with the genocide of the Native American population. Although it was part of the Creator's plan that Europeans should migrate to America, they were not meant to eradicate the Native Americans. The red coloration is connected with this nevertheless. The American continent suffers from slaughter of all kinds: of human beings, of great herds of bison and also of doves. The Europeans caused the slaughter of unbelievable numbers of living creatures. This bloodbath was prefigured, you can say, in the coloration of the red oak.

WW: But this would suggest that the slaughter of Native Americans and bison *was* envisaged in the plan. Surely this can't be so.

Oakbeen: It was there as a possibility. It was not inevitable. Nevertheless the Native Americans had to make way for the advancing civi-

lization of the white man, and the spilling of blood can be implicit in this. But slaughter was not necessary. It was the tragic destiny of their race to almost vanish from the face of the earth, but this is no excuse for your cruel acts. I want to stress this in the strongest terms!

WW: Why do the red oak's acorns grow so big?

Oakbeen: Because in North America almost everything is bigger than in Europe. Size is an intrinsic aspect of this continent.

WW: Why do they only ripen in the second year?

Oakbeen: Native Americans had no pigs so they didn't need acorns every year.

WW: What kind of answer is that?

Verena Staël von Holstein: I can't help it. That's her answer.

WW: Are there no other reasons?

Verena Staël von Holstein: It's a pretty daft reply.

Oakbeen: No, not really.

WW: Alright then, let's leave it. But why is the bark of the red oak fairly smooth compared with that of the common oak?

Oakbeen: The red oak is much younger than the common oak, as a conceived tree.

WW: Red oaks are very well suited to our large cities since they can survive severe air pollution and road salting unharmed. Why can they do this?

Oakbeen: Because the red oak is younger. Its life forces are stronger and younger, and — like the birch — it can cope with almost anything. The red oak also has a somewhat birch-like character, though not so pronounced as the birch itself. It has more youthful life force than the common oak. It is the youngest of the oaks and that's why it can survive better in large cities.

WW: Many thanks.

Oakbeen: You're welcome. It was fun.

WW: Is there anything else you'd like to say?

Oakbeen: Protect the trees!

The Pomegranate

Punica granatum

WW: Is there anyone who would like to speak for the pomegranate?

Verena Staël von Holstein: Zuleika.

WW: Hello Zuleika. Why does the pomegranate have such a tough shell?

Zuleika: It is very hot where I grow, and the hard shell protects my fruit and juice from drying out.

WW: Inside your fruit there are many chambers containing numerous angular seeds surrounded by a jelly-like, juicy, red flesh. Can you tell me anything about this flesh and the seeds. What is their task and why are they like this?

Zuleika: Originally the seeds exist, of course, to create new pomegranate trees. The fruit flesh is not just a reddish colour

but a really dark red, with jelly-like consistency. There are people who greatly enjoy the juice from this flesh. If you eat the seeds, they usually pass right through the stomach as they are tough and indigestible, but not at all poisonous.

Evoking a tender mood

WW: The juice has a slightly sour but also bitter, astringent kind of taste, but is very refreshing.

Zuleika: The pomegranate is a very ancient aphrodisiac. In ancient Persian culture the pomegranate was given to women  as a love gift, to evoke a tender mood in them. This is partly due to the colour — red is the colour of love — but also the beguiling taste. This juice might also invoke a mood of annoyance, but is more likely to have a positive effect. The pomegranate is not necessarily sweet but has an especially fruity quality, which makes people less deaf.

WW: How do you mean?

Zuleika: It helps you listen better to the body, while the spirit is somewhat suppressed. In other words, clear thoughts are pushed to one side a little, creating a mood that is not averse to love play. Tuning too strongly to conceptual life does not enhance love. A thought-suppressing mood is more appropriate.

At the same time the pomegranate has a beautiful shape and its colour reminds you of red gold. The chambers in my interior — as the ancient Persians also saw it — are like  little babies in my womb. This is why the pomegranate was also thought to enhance fertility.

WW: No doubt this is also why the pomegranate was formerly often mentioned in association with a woman's beauty.

Zuleika: Yes.

Leading a nation

WW: The pomegranate is often mentioned in the Old Testament. For instance Saul, the first king of Israel, was said to have sometimes lived under a pomegranate tree (Samuel I, 14:2). What does this mean?

Zuleika: You can't take it in a literal sense. He had no grove of pomegranates nor did he sleep beneath a pomegranate tree. But in his inner life, in meditation, he invoked a pomegranate in order to attain the state and essence of this tree. People often speak of someone sitting under a fig tree once he has achieved a particular level of initiation. But the level of the fig tree and that of the pomegranate are entirely different. This is also one of the reasons why every human has a personal tree — so that it can help him to reach a particular meditative tree level.

WW: What stage does the pomegranate correspond to?

Zuleika: This is the level of watching over a tribe or nation, with the capacity to lead a nation. This can also be a family, though, depending on the extent to which one can inwardly structure and form this group. This level also symbolizes fertility and propagation of a group. Once you achieve the level of the pomegranate tree you can have an overview of the sequence of incarnations of a group, as well as the reproductive sequence of a whole tribe.

WW: A tribal leader in those days therefore had to invoke in himself a spiritual state corresponding to the pomegranate tree in order to be able to lead his people?

Zuleika: Yes, especially if these people had the task of developing particular physical attributes. For this purpose individuals had to be brought together in a way that could give rise to a certain type of body.

Release from the tribe

WW: In Greek mythology the pomegranate was assigned to the gods of the underworld — to Hades and Persephone. Why?

Zuleika: Persephone always had to spend a third of the year in the underworld. The ancient Greeks no longer felt tribal existence to be appropriate. The last period of permissible tribalism was the era of Gabriel before our current Michael period. Nevertheless such ideas repeatedly surface in humanity. At such times the level of initiation correspond-ing to the pomegranate tree is a very desirable condition. Today, in the present state of soul, people tend to regard such a condition with some scepti-cism. Humanity's future lies in release from everything of a tribal nature, from all physical inheritance, and in seeking soul connection and relatedness. A further step will be spirit relat-edness. Spiritual relations will give rise to a kind of higher tribe, though released from all physical inheritance. The latter will transform and in future occur in a very different way.

Persephone

WW: Let us return to Greek mythology for a moment. The god of the underworld Hades seized Persephone and took her away from her mother into the underworld. Zeus decided that the girl might return to her mother as long as she had eaten nothing in the underworld. Shortly before she returned, Hades pressed six pomegranate seeds into her mouth, and she therefore had to reign in the underworld with Hades for a third of each year, spending the other two thirds above with her mother Demeter. What is meant by this story?

Zuleika: He imprisoned her in his tribe or clan. By eating the pomegranate seeds she becomes entwined with Hades and must spend a third of the year in the underworld. She did not eat the whole fruit, for then she would have been compelled to spend all her time in the underworld. In mythology Hades is seen as the clan of the underworld. Persephone comes back to the upper world in a semi-befuddled state and must as it were leave a third of herself behind in the underworld — the seeds of the plant, but not the leaf and blossoms. With Demeter, Persephone stands for fertility: the seeds rest over winter as forces in the ground, so as to absorb underworld forces, the soil's mineral forces. This is embodied in the pomegranate as symbol of tribal consciousness.

Making sexuality conscious

WW: Paris of Troy ended the quarrel between the goddesses Hera, Athene and Aphrodite by giving Aphrodite a golden apple or pomegranate. What symbolism lies here?

Zuleika: The legends of the Greeks derived from Persian legends, in which the European apple scarcely figures. Jewish legends are similar, such as that of Adam and Eve in paradise. This does not relate to an ordinary apple either but to a pomegranate, from which everything tribal emerges. Now listen: by opening up and eating the apple — they did not bite into it — they raised their sexuality into awareness in such a way that they perceived and understood the significance of reproduction for the future of the human race.

WW: So the breaking open and eating of the pomegranate is a process of awareness of sexuality and reproduction?

Zuleika: Once you understand the pomegranate, which symbolizes the fruit of the body, the moment you open it up, you recognize the secrets of sexuality and reproduction. This is why the pomegranate became the symbol of the tribe in meditation.

Love is red

This knowledge would be very important for the Oberufer paradise Play (an old play from southern Germany, performed at Christmas). Performances wrongly show the European apple, whereas the pomegranate should really hang on the tree. People should view the pomegranate in a more all-embracing way, also in relation to its red colour, which indicates Mars. People should ask themselves why love is red and has Mars qualities.

WW: Why does it?

Zuleika: This relates to the battle of the sexes, invoked in human relationships, in sexuality and love. By grasping hold of sexuality prematurely, people entered into strife with one another, into an enforced one-sidedness: women had to bear children while men must till the fields etc. This immediately laid the ground for a battle between the sexes, which initially took place in an archaic way: whenever one sex did the tasks of the other, or was not allowed to do so, it engaged in conflict with the other sex.

Because of this it is very important to understand the image and symbolism, the inner characteristics of the pomegranate.

WW: And what is the significance of the pomegranate in Greek mythology in relation to the Trojan war? Is it a symbol of renewed tribalism?

Zuleika: No, really the opposite. The Greeks already had problems with the Gabrielic tribal quality, for they were predisposed to live in a way in which tribal clans were no longer appropriate. When Paris gives the pomegranate as a gift to the goddess of love, this is tantamount to an act of liberation. It is symbolic of the fact that people should gradually emancipate themselves from tribal qualities. If Paris had given the pomegranate to Athene or Hera, he would instead have remained embedded in the tribe. Of course other things play into the Trojan war as well.

Integration in a spiritual community

WW: In Christian symbolism, the pomegranate symbolizes the
community of the faithful. Does this make sense?

Zuleika: Of course. This too is simple. It is archetypally Christian
after all that, as Christ says, one cannot enter the kingdom
of heaven without foreswearing father, mother and child and
becoming a disciple of Christ. This refers to the transformed
tribe, the spiritual tribe of the faithful, which is no longer
based on ties of blood.

Mathis Gothart Grünewald: Mary and Jesus (Stuppach Madonna)

WW: In a painting by Matthias Grünewald, Jesus is playing with a pomegranate given to him by his mother. This is meant to show that Mary is the mother of the Church. Is that right?

Zuleika: No.

WW: So what does this express?

Zuleika: Grünewald was one of the few painters to create spiritually true paintings. When Jesus plays with the pomegranate this shows that he is raising himself above the physical, tribal level, and is not subject to it. He thus shows that emancipating yourself from the tribe is a noble aim, enabling you to consciously enter a new spiritual community. This is voluntary affiliation with a spiritual community not tied to physical inheritance: allegiance solely to one's own I in emulation of Christ.

WW: Doesn't the pomegranate also symbolize the community of the faithful, though, as the Catholic Church sees it?

Zuleika: The Catholic Church tried to interpret all symbols in a way that served its own ends, but this should not be viewed too narrowly. Besides which, symbols should not be over-interpreted.

WW: What is the human trait that corresponds to you as pomegranate?

Zuleika: Forming communities. Human efforts to form a community and stay faithful to it; to remain faithful to your spiritual home.

WW: Is there anything more you'd like to say?

Zuleika: Stay true to your spiritual aims!

WW: Many thanks.

Zuleika: You're welcome.

The Soapberry

Sapindus mukorossi

WW: Is there anyone who can speak for the soapberry?

Verena Staël von Holstein: This probably won't be a problem since a number of experiments are being done with these trees in Europe.

    The name may sound a bit corny, but here is Indira, the soapberry.

WW: Hello Indira.

Indira: Morning.

WW: The so-called soapberries are indigenous to northern India and Nepal, and their fruits have been used for centuries as wash-nuts, for washing clothes. This tree can grow up to twenty-five metres in height and the girth of its trunk can reach five metres. Can you tell us a little about this tree?

Indira: Of course I can, for I am this tree. We are a very ancient and useful plant, which the Nepalese and northern Indians have used for centuries. They noticed that if these trees were standing by a river and the nuts fell into the water, this created

foam. Since then the shells of our fruits have been used for washing.

Our fruits contain small, spherical black seeds, from which new trees grow. When wet, the shell is highly sticky and even sugary, and this is what nourishes the seeds. People don't usually crack the nuts, but they fall on the soil and germinate, fed by the sugar content. In other words we supply our seeds with the right energy and nourishment to grow. We belong to the Sapindus genus. What else would you like to know?

WW: Please tell me something about the smell of your nuts.

Indira: Actually the soapberry hardly has any smell — just slightly sour and earthy. Its aroma is very unobtrusive. If you use these nuts for washing their smell evaporates straight away, and your washing will be completely free of odour afterwards.

No one likes the taste of soap in their mouth

WW: What substance in the shells has this washing capacity?

Indira: To put it very simply: soap. The scientific word for this is saponin. Soap is composed of glucose esters and saponification occurs when you esterify alcoholic substances. This is what occurs in our nutshells and enables us to protect our seeds against parasites. No one likes the taste of soap in their mouth, and this goes for insects as well.

WW: This sounds pretty logical, and as a human being I'm immediately inclined to ask why all trees don't do this.

Indira: Trees are very diverse. You might just as well assume that all trees should be pomegranates, for

they would all like to be the tree of paradise. But we took the soap-forming niche. Other trees have other qualities that enable them to protect themselves. Some defend themselves with tough wood, some through different ways of forming fruit or seeds; some trees actually want insects for pollination and dissemination etc. The multiplicity of creation is expressed in the diversity of different trees.

WW: Please tell me how to wash clothes with your nuts.

Indira: The best way is to grind them or at least break them up, as the outer shell is water-resistant. It has to be because otherwise our surroundings would turn soapy every time it rained. Then, when you're washing, the water washes the  soap out of the broken surfaces of the shell. Our kind of soap is very good for washing off organic substances and grease. It isn't so good for getting rid of non-organic substances. Synthetic lubricants and biro stains are harder to get rid of.

WW: Does washing with your nuts have any disadvantages?

Indira: No. You can use them in washing machines, and people with allergies don't have problems with them. They don't leave non-degradable residues in the water either. Nature copes very easily with what remains, and residues in the washing machine can simply be thrown out of the window.

Ritual washing

WW: Why are there trees that produce detergents?

Indira: Firstly because they wish to protect their seeds. In addition, we are Indians. Indian culture has a tradition of people purifying themselves in rivers. In former times Indians believed that the river Indus flowed directly from paradise and was therefore a divine river. That's why Indians ritually wash them-

selves in rivers, also the Ganges. Indians would prefer to bury all their dead in a river. A tree that produces detergent has a natural relationship with a human culture that is so devoted to washing in rivers. That's why detergent-bearing trees could really only develop in India. Ritual washing also served primarily to gain inner cleanliness as an approach towards nirvana conditions.

It is important that you understand this very ancient Indian cultural impetus, which is really very much older than Christianity. It is equally important for you to grasp that this ancient Indian cultural impulse is connected with our nuts.

WW: Could the soapberry also be cultivated here in Europe?

Indira: Absolutely.

WW: Would that be a good idea?

Indira: Yes and no. It would be good if you need a great many of our nuts. On the other hand, the tree tenders here would not be happy with great plantations of soapberry trees in Europe, as indigenous nature spirits find it hard to get used to new entities.

The need for cleanliness

WW: Is there a human quality that corresponds to you?

Indira: The need for cleanliness, above all of an inner kind. We correspond to the need of the Indian people to keep themselves pure, by which I really mean soul purity.

WW: So in a way you are a kind of religious tree ...

Indira: I am. Although I am not indigenous here, the undines are very pleased if you use my nuts to wash your clothes. You can also use them for washing your hair, indeed you can wash everything with them.

WW: How could I wash my hair with you?

Indira: Break me into pieces and agitate the water until it foams. Actually it's better if you grind up a handful of me and cook the fragments for ten minutes to make a soapy brew; that's a good shampoo.

The Frankincense

Boswellia sacra

Gunda: My name is Gunda.
WW: Hello Gunda.
Gunda: Hello Wolfgang. What would you like to know?
WW: Everything.
Gunda: Fire away.

Very strongly connected with the world of spirit

WW: Why are you such a small and many-branched tree with a papery bark?

Gunda: It is necessary for us to have many branches to tune to all aspects of the world of spirit. The more your branches divide, the more diverse are the regions into which you can enter. This is one reason for our many branches. The soil conditions are very tough where we live, which means there are times when we cannot produce leaves. That is why we draw into ourselves everything of a transient nature and form a strongly gnarled and knotty trunk. The papery bark is something you're already familiar with in your regions, since the birch has something similar. This bark shows that spirit beings expressed themselves through this type of paper in primeval times. And so we are a tree very strongly connected to the world of spirit. We are not necessarily a sacred tree, but are still very closely connected with the spiritual world. There's a difference.

Founders of religion in the Middle East

WW: How does this closeness to the spirit express itself? Why is this a stronger aspect in you than in other trees?

Gunda: Because we live in regions where the climate and conditions have given rise to a very developed capacity for openness to the world of spirit. It is not for nothing that we grow roughly in the areas where Christ once walked the earth. The Arabian peninsula is a region where the great founders of religions descended to earth. It is a place particularly favourable for religious impulses and gaining direct access to the spiritual world. It's here that the three great literate religions of Judaism, Christianity and Islam arose. It is here

Arabian peninsular (satellite image)

that Moses, Christ and Muhammad walked the earth, and also where mineral oil stalks today — for many people currently the most important energy-bearer and economic factor. Fossil oil is the cause of many great wars.

WW: What is so spiritually open about the Middle East and the Arabian peninsula that these three great religious founders incarnated there? Why didn't they incarnate in Europe for instance?

Gunda: There is too much water in Europe, giving rise to a quite different energy. While the Arabian peninsula is extensively surrounded by water too, through the proximity of the Mediterranean, the Nile and the Red Sea, water does not really penetrate this region. In the Holy Land there is only the river Jordan with Lake Galilee and the Dead Sea — one fresh water and the other salt. The Dead Sea is so salty that no life can really survive there. The Arabian peninsula is the centre from which the global dynamic of our current stage of earthly development proceeds — in other words, the stage which formed the current continents. You have to imagine the Arabian peninsula as the place this dynamic emanates from, even if the continental plates supposedly suggest something different. In spiritual terms this is the truth.

WW: Let's just reiterate: the Arabian peninsula, right up to the Holy Land, is the central point where all the plate tectonics of our earth are focused?

Gunda: Yes indeed, but only from a spiritual perspective.

WW: But why the Arabian peninsula particularly?

Gunda: In pictorial terms, the Holy Land is the place which the highest being chose for descending to earth. This event already exerted an influence before it occurred: it was long in preparation and the other founders of religions participated in the process. The summation of all human activity is focused in a very small region — mountains, desert, fresh water, salt water from Lake Galilee through the desert to the high mountains. It is all very compactly united in the one area of the Holy Land.

But the whole Arabian peninsula down to the Yemen and

also Egypt and Somalia is part of this region, as is the Nile, the Red Sea and, on the other side, Mesopotamia, today's Iraq, through to the Tigris and Euphrates. This whole region is involved. In a certain sense paradise was located in the region between the Tigris and Euphrates. Buddha was born somewhat further away. All other founders of the major religions lived in quite close geographical proximity, albeit at different times.

Not too much frankincense

The burning of frankincense resin puts people into a spiritual state in which they can perceive religious truths. This is why the frankincense tree grows in the area we have been speaking of.

WW: Can you describe this more precisely? What exactly happens when someone places dried frankincense resin on a red-hot coal so that frankincense smoke rises and people breathe it in?

Gunda: The resin burns and oxidizes. This means that it connects with the oxygen in the air. Oxygen is the bearer of the etheric and thus of life. Nitrogen is the bearer of astrality,  and carbon of the spirit. The astral nitrogen mediates between oxygen and carbon. As bearer of life, oxygen unites with the resinous substances in frankincense, giving off smoke. The smoke in turn renders the airy element visible and can thus reach the human being.

You can also eat frankincense resin and then it has more or less the same effect. Frankincense is very good for tooth pain, for instance, and acts as an antiseptic. You should not eat too much of it, though, as you might faint. So please just chew frankincense in small quantities, maybe when you get an attack of migraine. In this case, place frankincense crystals in your mouth and chew them (only in small amounts!). And you must use pure frankincense, not mixed with other substances. Then frankincense makes you incredibly free.

WW: What is the process involved when you chew frankincense resin?

Gunda: You free the etheric oils within it, releasing them through the mechanical action of grinding them with your teeth. These etheric oils connect directly with your blood, similar to the way they enter you through the lungs as incense in a church. The effect of this is that the I or ego as archetypally healthy aspect of your being can work in your blood to invoke health. Frankincense works in exactly this way on sick areas of the body. At the same time it opens people to impressions from the world of spirit, specifically religious impressions.

WW: What exactly do you mean by religious?

Gunda: Religiosity is a soul activity that mediates between the purely spiritual and the earthly. It seeks to lead what is purely earthly to recognize its spiritual sources more clearly. Which specific spiritual sources are meant here is less important — you can burn frankincense in Islamic religion, in Catholic religion and in the Christian Community just as well as you could have in ancient Egypt. It invariably opens people up so that, in your human physical body, you can perceive your spiritual origins.

Frankincense drives out demons

WW: Does burning frankincense at home also have a cleansing effect?

Gunda: Yes, this is very effective, for it invokes hierarchical beings who can bring about healing. Phantoms, spectres and demons cannot endure the presence of angels and are driven away by the frankincense smoke through which a spiritual opening occurs. A similar thing happens to your own inmost black thoughts. As human beings you are very capable of producing demons yourselves.

WW: How often should one do this at home, without doing it too much?

Gunda: Once a month would be a good average. You can also of course burn frankincense as an antiseptic measure if people in a house have been suffering from colds. However it isn't good to burn incense every day at home, as a home is not a church. The uninterrupted presence of hierarchical beings in a person's daily living quarters would inhibit his practical daily life and draw him away from his normal affairs.

Memories of the night sky's starry dome

WW: Let us return to the shape of your tree: why are your leaves lightly serrated, downy on both sides and so soft?

Gunda: It scarcely rains in the areas where I grow, but there is dew instead. The down on our leaves draws the dew from  the atmosphere, giving us an additional source of water. But in fact we need a great deal of water as we need a great deal of life. If you subscribe to religious truths this has an effect on your physical body, giving it a certain softness in the respiratory area. That's why our leaves are so soft. Really it would seem more appropriate for us to have very hard, tough leaves. But we can't because we are continually in contact with angels.

WW: Why are your blossoms so small, star-shaped and pale yellow?

Gunda: They look almost like lupin blossoms or horse chestnut candles but are much smaller. The horse chestnut has already told you something about its candles, and that the form of its blossoms does indeed reflect altar candles. And  since each person has a star, and every star is a dwelling place of the hierarchies, all the small blossoms on our umbel recall the night sky's starry dome, as the place where human egos reside.

Song turned to substance

WW: If I cut a slit in a frankincense tree the resin would dry in a tear-shaped lump in the air. What is happening here?

Fruit

Gunda: Tear-shaped — so you see I'm crying! In principle it's the same as when rubber trees or maple trees are tapped. But the resin of the frankincense, by contrast, has the capacity to invoke angels. I give up the resin as sacrifice and let it emerge for human use. This is self-sacrifice on my part, as I give away something of my angel-invoking power. The resin of the frankincense tree is thus song turned to substance. When you sing you also call on the angels, so you can see the clear connection between both.

The muezzin as representative of the Islamic religion in the regions where I grow also sings: he calls on the faithful and the angels.

WW: In former times frankincense was even more precious than today, or was regarded as more precious. There is a legend, or it may be a true story, about the Egyptian pharaoh Hatsheput's journey to the country of Punt, which is probably Somalia. In the New Testament, too, there is the story of the Three Kings who brought gifts to Jesus, including frankincense. Why was frankincense so highly regarded in those times?

Gunda: Frankincense was as precious as gold — it was weighed against gold: a grain of gold against a grain of frankincense. It was extremely hard to obtain frankincense, very laborious, as can be imagined when you consider the conditions under which we grow. There were no transport helicopters in those days, but instead our resin was brought to the coast with great difficulty by transporting it in frankincense caravans through thief-infested terrains and deserts, for instance on the famous frankincense trail. In those days frankincense caravans were often attacked because they bore such a precious commodity.

This is why our resin was so expensive and precious. At the same time the three precious substances gold, frankincense and myrrh are connected with the human being's three basic powers of thinking, feeling and will. Gold corresponds to thinking, frankincense to feeling and myrrh to action.

Striving heavenwards

WW: Nowadays frankincense grows as a tree in southern Arabia and Somalia, at heights of 1000 to 1800 metres, and the places where it is cultivated are a carefully guarded secret.

Gunda: This is because frankincense is still valuable. As long as all the world's churches use frankincense for religious purposes, and are still reliant on it in their rites, it will remain a continual source of wealth. It won't go out of fashion. And frankincense is still not easy to grow, so this hasn't changed. This tree also strives heavenwards: the higher its location, the better it will grow in principle.

WW: The ancient Egyptians tried to cultivate frankincense trees in Egypt. Why didn't they succeed?

Gunda: Because it was much too dark in the Nile valley.

WW: Why too dark? It isn't especially shady there, and light penetrates everywhere!

Frankincense trees in Dhofar (Oman)

Gunda: The light doesn't penetrate as easily into the Nile valley as at higher altitudes, which I need. The Nile valley is down below, and light takes longer to get down there. On mountains I am nearer to light. Apart from that the soil is different in the Nile valley: it is floodland for the most part. The ancient Egyptians could have cultivated us if they had tried doing so at higher altitudes, but this didn't occur to them.

WW: Why is one meant to tap the frankincense tree on the hottest days of the year to harvest resin?

Gunda: Because the world of spirit works most immediately in the flame, whose other image is heat. Heat is the only elemental entity that people can experience both inwardly and outwardly. The flame is the visible manifestation of heat, and in a flame you have a direct experience of the spiritual world. On the hottest day of the year, even in purely physical terms, the spiritual world is most immediately present. This means that frankincense obtained on this day also leads you most directly to the world of spirit. The connection is really quite simple.

Remedy for anxiety

WW: If you inhale frankincense smoke this is meant to help against asthma. Is this true?

Gunda: Frankincense has an antiseptic effect and combats all illnesses connected in some way with anxiety. Asthma is one such illness. Frankincense smoke also combats Crohn's disease since this is also connected with fear. The other effect — which you are aware of because you are chewing frankincense right now — is that it leads to clarity of thought and frees up the respiratory tract. You can also eat frankincense if you are prone to anxiety attacks.

The quality of frankincense is deteriorating

WW: Has the quality of frankincense changed in recent times?

Gunda: Very definitely! Politicization of the region where we grow, and the creation of hollows and cavities where mineral oil is extracted, has brought about changes throughout the region, and decisively affected frankincense. It would be good if people were to cultivate frankincense plantations in Australia.

WW: Why there particularly?

Gunda: Because Australia is so innocent.

WW: But isn't it a principle of the frankincense tree that it should specifically grow in the regions which form the hub of tectonic and religious impulses today? This isn't in Australia.

Gunda: Australia will gain importance, as will the whole region of South-East Asia, also economically. The ahrimanic forces entering the Arabian peninsula through extraction of oil there will spoil and unbalance what was formerly paradise and the points of entry there for the spirit. This will also impact on frankincense. Mineral oil contains the earth's powers of memory. This is something Kapuvu, the Stone One, described in your previous conversations. The moment that mineral oil is traded in this region for purely egotistic and ahrimanic reasons, these impulses have a dramatic effect on plants growing on the earth's surface, disrupting their connection with the world of spirit. The quality of Arabian frankincense will therefore continue to deteriorate.

WW: Can you be a little more explicit about this?

Gunda: More explicit?

WW: Yes: how is the quality of frankincense changing?

Gunda: Many people have already noticed that the quality of the aroma of frankincense has changed. This means that people can no longer open themselves so easily to the world of spirit through the agency of frankincense. The etheric quality of frankincense is primarily what induces this. If you burn peppermint or other herbs, their smoke will give rise to other experiences. Because the composition of frankincense is changing, through the strong influx of ahrimanic powers where mineral oil is extracted, spiritual opening to spiritual truths is not so easy as it once was. The longer this process continues, the worse the quality of frankincense will become.

WW: Is there a human quality corresponding to the frankincense tree?

Gunda: The power of faith.

WW: Thank you. Is there anything else you would like to say?

Gunda: I would like to remind people in central Europe that they too can do something to counteract the oil wars, for instance by praying. Do it!

Palo Santo

The Palo Santo or Vera Wood

Bulnesia arborea

WW: I am just lighting a splinter of wood from the palo santo tree in Bolivia or Peru; it will keep glimmering, releasing a pleasant scent. This is how people use such splinters in the countries where the tree grows, believing that the smoke drives away evil spirits. Can you see if you can contact this tree?

Verena Staël von Holstein: Miller can do this, for he sensed the smoke here in the mill when you lit a splinter before.

Miller: I can find a connection, but this tree is very far away.

WW: Does it have a name?

Miller: Paolo.

A descendant from paradise

WW: Can you say anything about this palo santo (sacred wood) tree?

Miller with Paolo: It is the remnant of a descendant from paradise. In very ancient times it was brought from the Himalayas with people who migrated to South America, as they needed it there. They needed it to avoid falling sick on the new continent. Naturally the tree adapted to the new conditions; but awareness remained that this wood can dispel evil spirits, and above all illnesses. The tree does not grow excessively tall and is not particularly striking. It has green leaves and hard wood. The strange thing about this tree is that it ought really to bear needles.

Healing forces from the time of paradise

WW: This wood is used not by burning it completely but by lighting shavings or splinters that smoulder and give off a fragrance. Can you say anything about what happens during this moment?

Miller with Paolo: This releases the healing forces of pre-conscious epochs of humanity. The wood corresponds to human qualities before the Fall occurred — that is, the state of paradise. This ancient quality is sealed in the wood and has a particularly strong effect on rooms. Because the essence of this tree is limited in scope, it works best if confined within a space or environment that does not extend too far. It tries to fill the same space that it previously extended into as a tree with the powers of its smoke and fragrance. If you use this wood to spread fragrance, this acts as a spiritual disinfectant, dispelling all negative forces.

WW: So it's just like frankincense!

Miller with Paolo: Yes, but at a different level. Frankincense drives out spirits at a spiritual level but palo does not do this. Instead it dispels them at the level of life, just beyond the physical level.

WW: Can you explain this more precisely?

Miller with Paolo: Palo santo does this in the realm in which your personal body elemental works — in the life forces which directly connect your physical body with your etheric body. With the smoke from the palo santo tree you have an opportunity to create a state such as that in which human beings lived in paradise. Working out of these healthy life forces, the tree can still influence the sphere of life in human beings today, above all in rooms and houses; for houses protect your etheric as well as your physical body.

WW: I'd like to examine this a little more closely. Let's assume we have a house in which various demons might be living. On the one hand we have frankincense, and on the other palo santo. Let's imagine we light both at once. Please can you explain the different ways in which frankincense and palo santo drive out these spirits?

Miller: I don't need the tree to tell you that, I can tell you myself. This is something you asked about very precisely, here in the mill on a previous occasion, in relation to doubles. There are different doubles that work within different regions of the human being, for instance in the physical, etheric or astral. There are always obstructions at certain soul, etheric or physical levels. If you have beings that are tending to eat away at the human being, causing illness — that is, in the etheric realm — then palo santo is especially beneficial. Frankincense is effective in dispelling beings that are more related to soul nature. Ideally, therefore, you would burn both in a house, for each dispels different kinds of being. You make yourself healthier physically if you burn palo santo, and you also make things easier for me as house spirit if you keep your house healthy.

Your personal body elemental is very enthusiastic about this wood. If you burn palo santo, the elemental can absorb an archetypal image of the human being in paradise, mediated by the smoke, and connect it with your current condition.

Frankincense, in contrast, speaks more to your soul and even your I, since it resists demons and phantoms. But you can also see an ordinary cold as an attack by a being — for a being is associated with every illness, and this is the level at which palo santo works.

The Inca initiates and their healing influence in smoke

WW: Can you tell me any more about this tree? What does it emanate in the mountains of Peru when it grows there?

Miller with Paolo: It emanates healing forces. It is noticeable that people there are relatively healthy despite the harsh climate. Above all this tree once supported the elevated, health-bestowing culture of the Incas. Inca initiates still knew how to use this wood to alter human physical bodies with the smoke. If they were real initiates they were able to heal people with palo santo smoke, but also intervene in physical bodies to alter their condition.

WW: Can you give an example of this?

Miller with Paolo: Let's take a simple example. If someone broke their arm, and an initiate was nearby, he made the palo santo smoke so thick that the person with the broken arm lost consciousness. Then, via this smoke, the initiate could enter the human being and mend the broken bone with his forces. This is because the archetypal form of the healthy human being was implicit in the smoke. People don't have this ability any more — you would have to undergo very laborious stages of initiation. Inca initiation has faded to a shadow of what it once was.

WW: So this wood really is a proper healing wood.

Miller with Paolo: Yes, but only if you know how to work with it.

WW: You mean that someone who uses it has to have the right stance?

Miller with Paolo: Yes. All participants must of course be of a white magic persuasion, for the moment any black magic enters these processes, enormous damage could be done with this wood — as always in such cases.

WW: Do some people do this intentionally?

Miller with Paolo: Yes. Particularly in South America they have a custom of using various smoke-induced conditions in connection with destructive forces. However it is not easy to use palo santo for destructive purposes. You have to be a fairly capable black magician. Palo santo protects itself to a large degree.

WW: Is there anything more we should say about this wood?

Miller: I as House Spirit would like to say that everyone ought to burn a stick of palo santo wood once a year in his house. And the tree itself says:

Palo: Retain your original innocence!

WW: Is that the human quality corresponding to this tree?

Miller with Paolo: Definitely.

Miller: But remember that this tree does not exist in huge quantities. You shouldn't start ordering large amounts of its wood, and thus endanger its survival. It really would be enough to burn it just once a year.

The song of Vera, or truth

WW: There's an old legend relating to palo santo. Can you tell me anything about this?

Miller with Paolo: An ancient chieftain from the region where Columbia and Venezuela are located today had a daughter named Vera, whose name means truth. This is important! The daughter was very beautiful and above all could sing very beautifully. All the young men in the area fell desperately in love with her because of this, and she fled away to the woods, but they followed her. They begged, if they might not marry her, that she would at least continue singing. Vera agreed, and to this day she still sings in the forests. This singing of Vera is expressed in the physical form of the palo santo tree.

WW: Is this just a legend or is there any truth in it?

Miller with Paolo: You can certainly say that this tree has a great deal to do with truth, for if you burn its wood it spreads a fragrance which enables beings of truth to enter, and dispels deceitful beings. So-called 'evil' beings can't endure the smell of palo santo, since it is connected with truth. The feathery character of the leaf of this tree is similar to that of the locust and, somewhat more distantly, to that of the ash. So you can

see that it absorbs a great deal of light. It is wholly given over to the light.

In addition this tree forms canopy -like crowns, which give great protection to creatures beneath. If you stand under a palo santo tree you will be protected from deceitful beings.

WW: Can you say any more about song and how it expresses itself in these trees?

Miller with Paolo: Since this tree doesn't grow in Europe you can't hear its song. But if you stand very quietly under the tree in South America, you can imagine you still hear Vera's singing

in its leaves. The leaves whisper, although not like the wittering of the poplar, that angel tree, but rather like a faraway song.

WW: Who is Vera — a group spirit of the palo santo, or something quite different?

Miller with Paolo: She was an initiate from Native American civilization who incorporated parts of her being into the palo santo tree. Perhaps one can describe her as a kind of tree nymph, although she was actually more than this.

WW: But she was once a human being?

Miller with Paolo: Yes, an initiate.

The sacrificing gesture of truth

WW: Why does this tree form such beautiful yellow flowers, which look like small, outward-opening spoons?

Miller with Paolo: They look like small, wide spoons and the petals are arranged as a pentagon. The colour of the

flower immediately reveals a connection with Jupiter, as does the pentagonal arrangement of the petals. The number five manifest here makes the palo santo

an image of the human being, who can form a pentagram with outstretched arms. This refers to the advanced, higher human being — really the human being who has formed his spirit self at the future stage of Jupiter, and who will or ought to live in love. This far-distant future is indicated in the colour of the flower and the arrangement of petals.

The upwards-opening, spoon-like shape of the petals expresses the sacrificing gesture of love, which flows back to the gods. Each of these petal spoons is a spoon full of truth for the gods.

WW: Why is this tree evergreen?

Miller with Paolo: That is nothing special, but just typical for the continent. In South America relatively large numbers of trees are evergreen and there is no leaf-fall as here in Europe. It is also a gift of the gods, who show that these trees can offer special protection.

WW: Is it true that palo santo enhances digestion and has a calming effect?

Miller with Paolo: The bark, when properly prepared, can act as a strong calmative remedy, and since restlessness in people often comes from the stomach region, palo santo promotes digestion, or calms you via the stomach. Here too you can see a connection with lies. If someone lies a lot, he also damages his stomach, and palo santo has a lie-dispelling effect. If you absorb palo santo you will find yourself less adept at lying.

WW: Is palo santo also effective against asthma and bronchitis?

Miller with Paolo: People with asthma and bronchitis feel very well in rooms where palo santo is burned, for asthma expresses a sensitivity to deceitfulness in the world. Palo santo can thus be turned into a useful medicine, although science and medicine have not yet taken this up. A narrower, traditional knowledge of herbalism still prevails. Homeopathy hasn't made use of palo santo either.

Wherever palo santo grows, people like placing this tree in tubs on terraces. People love palo santo because they feel protected in its presence, although this is normally an unconscious inkling.

Live your life in truth!

WW: The wood is yellowish and the core of the trunk is olive green to yellow. What does this colour express?

Miller with Paolo: The bark also has this olive-coloured tone, like the core of the trunk. Through the yellow of blossoms and wood, and the olive-green core, the forces of light unite with those of water. This interplay expresses a high degree of health, a connection between the light-filled Jupiter world and the watery earth world. That's why the wood has these 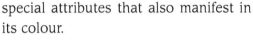 special attributes that also manifest in its colour.

WW: I'd like to return for a moment to the burning of palo santo wood as incense. What happens when you burn this fragrance in a room where someone is sitting? How does his inner stance change?

Miller with Paolo: Several things happen. First of all the person will become more receptive to truth. Of course there are people who are already very open to the truth. By sitting in palo santo smoke, such people undergo a kind of further development of their unconscious capacity to reject lies. Your attitude to lies changes when you inhale palo santo smoke, particularly in relation to lies in everyday life. Here we mean primarily the various roles people are stuck in today, so that they are not fully themselves or are even living a lie. Each person naturally has to reflect on this himself. When people sit in palo santo smoke, they begin to question the role of lies in their life, and allow truth to stream in and illuminate them. Which particular truth this might be is insignificant.

WW: But couldn't you say, then, that palo santo smoke is identical with frankincense, for this substance also protects us against the demons of untruth?

Miller with Paolo: Frankincense works with the human being's power of faith and belief, the astral realm of faith. Palo santo, in contrast, tends more in the direction of the human being's etheric realm. Palo santo says: live your life in truth! What the one does in the realm of life, the other does in the realm of feeling. This is a huge difference. You don't become more faithful and believing when you stand in a room where palo santo burns, although you certainly do in the presence of frankincense. In palo santo smoke you become more alive and more true, live more fully in truth. This might also be a mathematical truth, a realm where frankincense would be no use whatsoever, because it tends to diminish scientific thinking.

Lies are unmasked

WW: Does palo santo nevertheless counteract the demons of lies, in a way similar to frankincense?

Miller with Paolo: Very strongly. If you're preparing a meeting and you know that big liars are coming to it, you can put a spanner in their works by burning palo santo in the room beforehand. If you were to burn frankincense, this would be less effective.

WW: How can we see this in spiritual terms? Let us assume such a meeting takes place and that liars are present. What happens to the lie demons that such people have around them? Are they obstructed or suppressed by the palo santo smoke, or how should we view this?

Miller with Paolo: Smoke exists to make light and air more visible. The moment people peppered with lie phantoms enter the palo santo smoke, they start perceiving these phantoms in themselves. This is because light is more visible in the smoke, for normally it exists by being invisible. The physical smoke makes the light more visible; and the concealed spiritual ground behind it likewise renders the lie more visible. This makes it harder for someone to say something deceitful. Most people don't want their lies to come to light; normally they lie so that others don't notice. The moment something renders a lie visible, it is hindered and obstructed.

WW: And what happens to the liar himself if he enters a room where palo santo is burning?

Miller with Paolo: The liar begins to perceive his lies, although very deep-seated, ingrained lies, are only superficially affected. Such a person will be unaware of why he is becoming aware of his lies.

Miller: That's why we house spirits love palo santo smoke, as we don't wish to have any lies in our dwellings.

WW: It is often the case that a kind of etheric imprint of someone who has lived in a house for a longish period is left on the walls there. Maybe this also happens if someone enters a room just once. What happens to these etheric imprints if you burn palo santo?

Miller: If these are negative residues they are dispelled by the smoke. In this case the smoke beings quite specifically set about erasing these human residues. This occurs particularly if the smoke derives from a plant such as palo santo. If the imprints are good ones, by contrast, they are not fixed there by the smoke but nor are they affected. With other types of smoke this is sometimes different. There are in fact disinfectant or overlaying smoke qualities that can also expel the good and leave something sterile behind. Palo santo is more concerned with our sense of wellbeing as house spirits, and our etheric life becomes healthier through it. At the same time it drives out lies, by unmasking them.

The lies of the church and the Spaniards

WW: As long ago as the time of Columbus, Spaniards sent the wood of this tree back to Europe because they supposedly saw the Incas use it to combat syphilis. Is there any truth in this? And what happened to this wood and the smoke it gave off when it was brought to Europe?

Miller with Paolo: Naturally palo santo changed in nature when it was brought to Europe since it had to adapt to a new continent and beings in that continent.

There is something of fundamental importance in relation to syphilis, though. From a spiritual rather than a medical perspective this disease arose through the Catholic Church's deceitful relationship with morality. Its deceitful, mendacious and immoral stance was the spiritual breeding ground for the spread of syphilis. The widespread lack of morality of the Catholic Church at this time — manifest in popes having children yet preaching celibacy and other such things — created the basis for syphilis. On the other hand there was still a certain capacity for spiritual perception within the Catholic Church then, and people could sense that palo santo wood had an alleviating effect on syphilis. It helped, though it did not offer a complete cure.

In addition the Spaniards felt superior, and regarded Native Americans as sub-human. They felt themselves entitled to murder and destroy whatever crossed their path. At the same time they preached Christianity with missionary zeal, feeling that this was their duty.

When the wood of palo santo was brought to Europe, however, it lost much of its power because it was compelled to fight against the Spaniards' whole edifice of lies. This is why the tree did not spread in Europe. Other plants or vegetables such as potatoes, on the other hand, established themselves very quickly. Palo santo remains largely unknown in Europe.

WW: Can you tell me a little about how the conquering Spaniards perceived this palo santo smoke during their first military campaigns? Something must have occurred to draw their attention to the importance of this smoke.

Miller with Paolo: The conquistadores always took priests along with them. Catholic priests of a certain level of schooling were still to some extent initiates, or at least they had perceptions that this tree and thus also its wood, and the smoke emanating from it, had special significance. In the Bible too there are a good number of descriptions of people at particular levels of initiation sitting under trees.

And the Spaniards always had priests with them, both to ensure their own souls' salvation and to impose Christianity on these 'savages.' Among these priests were some with clairvoyant perception.

A second aspect was to do with economics, for frankincense was expensive and primarily came from areas that were difficult to reach. When the Spaniards observed that palo santo smoke was holy, they conceived the idea of replacing frankincense with palo santo from 'their own' regions. This was another aspect, but was not realized: higher initiates in Spain discovered that this palo santo smoke tended to unmask one's own lies, whereas frankincense did not have this effect.

The practice of cruelty was a free decision

WW: What did the Spaniards do to the indigenous South American population by eradicating or decimating them in such a brutal way?

Miller with Paolo: The main thing at stake here was gold. Gold was a ritual substance for the Incas. They were relatively highly developed and had an organized state and means of self-defence. When the Spaniards came and tried to take their gold — purely for non-ritual reasons, out of greed — the Incas defended themselves. They had a palo santo culture and therefore an accentuated capacity for unmasking lies, and so they could perceive the falsity of the Spaniards and the Catholic Church. For this reason the Catholic initiates felt compelled to murder at least the leading ranks of the Incas, for otherwise the Catholic Church would have made no headway there. In addition, the Spanish royalty wished to own a realm in which the sun never sets, and also wanted to rule over an entirely Catholic kingdom.

A great deal of blood was spilled in consequence and appalling acts of cruelty were committed by the Spaniards — all in the name of Christ, who of course does not condone such things.

From a higher perspective, all this also occurred to instigate a process of evolution. The South American population was not capable of introducing a process of development leading to the mind soul, let alone the consciousness soul. These peoples could not of themselves initiate such development, and Europeans were needed to do so. The mind soul first had to spread across the whole globe, and this cannot be overlooked when considering the cruelty that was practised. Yet these people of the mind soul had the freedom to act differently, and did not have to inflict this genocide on the population of South America.

WW: We always meet these seemingly irreconcilable contradictions: on the one hand a population incapable of developing a modern form of consciousness; and on the other, Europeans who instigate this evolutionary impetus but at the same time kill everyone around them. Was this inevitable? Could things have been done by more peaceful means?

Miller with Paolo: Clearly not, for until recently your freedom was not advanced enough to make such developments happen in a peaceful way. Since the Mystery of Golgotha, every event on earth is placed within the freedom of the ego or I. But people at the time we are speaking of were not able to go to a different country and leave the people living there in freedom. This created a karmic debt, which central Europeans shouldered as a whole. As their culture was flowering, the people of central and western Europe were unable to leave other people free. This means that all the cruel acts occurred in freedom. The spiritual world would gladly have seen a peaceful solution instead, if you could have found one. It must also be added that there were adversarial powers for whom these brutal acts were very convenient.

A rigid corset

WW: What changed on the South American continent through the fact that the Spaniards treated the indigenous people so brutally, and what are the continued repercussions of this? Many of the inhabitants of South America appear very passive, or somehow rootless; they seem to have little initiative, and lack a strong relationship with their natural surroundings. Is this way of life a consequence of the Spaniards' brutal intervention in their lives at that time?

Miller with Paolo: This is indeed one of the consequences of the Spaniards' brutal intervention in the life of the Incas and of other peoples, and it is connected with the fact that a rigid system of rules was imposed on the South American population. This severe pre-Lutheran Catholicism had a very rigid view of morality. And within the South American population no religious and spiritual revolution ever occurred in the same way as Luther brought about in central Europe, to break with the Catholic Church's rigid dictates. In a certain sense the people of South America still live within this pre-Lutheran Catholic system, and this is a problem that besets the South American continent to this day. That is also why the Pope holds such huge celebrations there.

WW: But I'm still surprised that many people there have no real relationship with their surroundings and with nature.

Miller with Paolo: This Catholic system from the fourteenth or fifteenth century also had no relationship with nature. People simply slipped into this system and have not yet emerged from it. You could say they are 500 or 600 years old.

WW: So they need some kind of reformation there?

Miller with Paolo: Absolutely.

Machu Picchu (Peru), Intihuatana

The tethered sun

WW: The Incas developed a well-organized administrative state between the thirteenth and sixteenth centuries, which used statistical records to ascertain and coordinate the needs of and services provided by the population. The people had to give a third of their working hours to Inti, the sun god, and a further third to the aristocracy, and were only allowed to retain a third of the yield of their own work. What kind of being was the sun god Inti?

Miller with Paolo: The sun god Inti was an image of the external sun, but one into which Michael and the Christ being had not yet entered. In those days therefore an ancient, monotheistic form of worship prevailed. The moment the sun was ensouled by the Christ being, it was no longer monotheistic but a part of

Execution by the Spaniards of the Inca king Atawallpa in 1533

the Trinity. The sun of the Incas remained Gabrielic as it were. The interesting thing about the Incas is that the sun always had to be tethered.

WW: Why?

Miller with Paolo: They had giant altars to which the sun was tethered so that it would not disappear during the night and in winter. Inca rites were very elevated, though, and took a perception of preparation for the advent of Christ very seriously. But then they remained stuck in this expectancy.

Unwilling to absorb something new

WW: Was this why, in expectancy of a god coming to them from over the sea, they believed that the invading Spaniards represented this divinity? Was this also the reason for the internecine war between the two Inca brothers Atahualpa and Huascar, when Pizarro landed in Peru in 1532?

Miller with Paolo: That was one of the reasons. Atahualpa always had a vision that a new light or stance of soul would come over from northern Europe. But others, such as his brother, were

Macchu Picchu (Peru)

not prepared to accept this idea. Similar outlooks have been preserved in these countries to this day, also expressed in the fact that people don't accept the indigenous Americans, but suppress them. Manifest in this continent is an attitude that is rooted in the past and is unwilling to absorb anything new.

WW: What is the significance of Machu Picchu, the well-preserved ruins of the Incas' city on the heights of the Andes in today's Peru?

Miller with Paolo: It was here that the sun was tethered on certain dates, and then released again at other times. Macchu Picchu was a very important and ancient sacred place of the sun — now seen as one of the seven wonders of the world. In fact there are several of these wonders on the American continent, such as the statue of Christ standing over the port of Rio. These two monuments reflect the contradictions and destiny of the South American continent: on the one hand the ancient sacred site of the Incas, on the other a more Catholic monument. But both encapsulate a tendency to look back to the past. Macchu Picchu had the task of preserving the old sun forces so they would not slip out of human beings' grasp.

WW: The Incas operated successfully on the human skull and in doing so used the trepanning technique. Can you tell me any more about this, and also whether palo santo played any part in it?

Miller with Paolo: In Inca operations palo santo smoke was always used, for all smoke — think of a smoked sausage — has a preserving or sterilizing effect. This is due to the ash remnants contained in the smoke. Ash is something dead. Death prevents decay, even if this sounds illogical; what has been deadened to a certain extent can no longer be corrupted. That's why the Incas used palo santo smoke in their surgery. You can see a connection here with ancient Egyptian surgical techniques, and the ancient Egyptians also had an ancient sun culture, with their sun god Ra. The Incas did not train people in this surgical technique but searched until they found someone capable of practising this kind of healing, who was then admitted to the circle of healers. There was no medical training as such.

The condor as image of the soul

WW: Why was the condor sacred to the Incas?

Miller with Paolo: The condor was the bird of the soul. This huge bird can fly very well. If you ever see a condor circling over the Andes, you'll notice how beautifully and capably it flies. It makes perfect use of the updraught thermals that rise under the cliffs of the Andes when the sun shines on them. They can ascend so high they can scarcely be seen by the human eye. For the Incas this was an image of the ascending soul disappearing into the heavens. They passed on this image to the non-initiated population, so that people might learn that their soul rises heavenwards like the condor, and must vanish into it.

Condor in the Andes

The black magician and the lie-detecting tree

WW: Why is it that a lie-detector tree such as the palo santo grows in South America but not in Europe? Or is there any such tree in Europe?

Miller with Paolo: The greatest black magician who ever lived came from central or southern America, and palo santo offered a certain counterweight and opposition to him. He was crucified on an upside-down cross at the time of the Mystery of Golgotha. This black magician was able to connect very strongly with the demons of deceit and corresponding higher beings of black magic. That is why this continent had to have a tree offering a certain protection against these dark forces. And so this special, anti-lie tree grows in South America, where this extremely powerful liar lived. There is no corresponding tree in Europe. Instead, in Europe, people use frankincense, which has a different kind of effect.

The Olive

Olea europaea

WW: The olive tree has been cultivated since the fourth century BC. Why has this tree played such an important role in so many people's lives?

Olivia: The olive tree is an energy bearer of special quality. In former times it was hard to feed people with fats, but you can obtain a pure fat or oil from me. This is why the olive tree was so important for people. It supplied pure fat in large quantities, and relatively easily. It therefore enormously enriched the supply of energy for human beings.

Golden oil

WW: Why does the olive tree have such strong and extensive roots, descending to a depth of six metres?

Olivia: This is like a vine, which also delves deep — in fact even deeper — into the soil. The olive absorbs all the underground forces, and from these draws the qualities it converts into its oil. If you planted an olive tree on a rubbish dump, it

would pass on the nature of the rubbish to its oil. The olive needs to penetrate the ground strongly with its roots. At the same time this is an embodiment of the olive's spiritual quality, and can act as an example to human beings of how they too should penetrate the earth.

In olden times people saw the oil of the olive tree as containing enormous sun forces. This is still true today but people no longer experience it. It is also this which gives rise to the beautiful colour of olive oil, a shimmering greeny gold through to almost pure gold. The oil has a low viscosity and an acerbic, bitter taste, which surprises many people. This tends towards the effect of myrrh, that is, towards will qualities. In olive oil you have a strongly fragrant aspect on the one hand, then a strongly golden aspect and also an astringent, myrrh-type aspect. This corresponds to all three realms of the human being — thinking, feeling and will. It is this that makes olive oil so special.

In addition, the olive tree can grow very old indeed, and therefore has a connection with various different spiritual eras of humanity. The quality of oil is still excellent in old trees, perhaps even better than in young ones.

WW: Europe's oldest olive tree is said to be about 2000 years old, and to grow in the city of Bar in Montenegro.

Olivia: That's right.

WW: Why is the shape of the olive so gnarled, why does the wood grow so slowly, and why does it branch so profusely?

Olivia: To survive. We have many branches for the same reason as the frankincense tree, because we wish to grasp as many aspects of

the spiritual realm as possible. We are gnarled so that we can survive a long time. We penetrate deeply into the earth in order to absorb all the forces residing there.

WW: Tradition has it that the more crooked and gnarled an olive tree is, the better the yield of olives and oil will be. Is this true?

Olivia: Yes.

WW: Why?

Olivia: The more time a tree has absorbed, the better it can produce oil.

WW: Why is the olive tree evergreen, and what dictates when leaves are discarded?

Olivia: The olive tree is green because it can unite all three powers we have mentioned. If you could do this you too would be evergreen and immortal. If the leaves are discarded at all, it is once their substance has been practically etherized or has dissolved. This usually occurs after several years, irrespective of the season. Then the tree puts forth new leaves.

Harmonious dimensions

WW: Can you say anything about the shape of your leaves?

Olivia: Unlike the frankincense tree, the leaves are very sturdy and dark green, but reflect the sun like a mirror so that they have a silvery sheen. The leaves are long and narrow, with a pointed, lancet-like tip. Their upper side is more green, their underside more silvery. The shape of the leaf is balanced so that all three tendencies are expressed in it too — a certain roundness, a certain length and at the same time a certain stability. The olive tree manifests harmonious dimensions. Today, when the prevailing cultural impetus is no longer centred in the Mediterranean area, the olive tree has altered somewhat, though it still continues to produce good oil. But in the fourth post-Atlantean cultural epoch, when humanity's civilization was still

rooted in the Mediterranean, the olive tree was the Yggdrasil.

WW: As far as I remember, Steiner says that in the Greek era human beings lived best and most harmoniously in their physical body, in a kind of perfect equilibrium.

Olivia: Definitely.

WW: And now the ash is the Yggdrasil?

Olivia: Yes, today the ash is the I-tree. The Yggdrasil is the central tree in Teutonic mythology, where it is designated as the ash. What I mean is that there has been a prevailing tree in every era that corresponded to the conditions of the time. In the fourth post-Atlantean cultural epoch, this was the olive tree, and now it is the ash.

WW: What can you tell me about the fruit and its hard kernel?

Olivia: The olive has no kernel but a stone. This is surrounded by the flesh of the olive, which is black, green or dark terracotta colours. The oil is contained in the flesh surrounding the stone, and pressing it releases the olive oil. The stone itself, though, is an image of the earth.

WW: Why can't you really eat an olive raw but only after repeated marinading in water?

Olivia: Because it is so bitter. But olives are mainly marinaded in brine, not in water. When they are pressed they are not marinaded first. Salt is the bearer of the I. The salt in the brine draws the bitterness out of the olive, which humans don't like. Bitter substances connect the human being very strongly with the earth — that's why you take a bitter remedy if you have digestive problems. Myrrh is bitter and works into human actions, into earth existence.

WW: What happens, from a spiritual perspective, when you press olives to obtain oil?

Olivia: When you press olives you separate the over-hard physical part from the fluid contained within it. This divides the physical from life, for fluid is the bearer of life and is separated from the aspect of death at pressing. A resurrection process is accomplished and furthermore a conjuring of the human being's resurrection body, but only prefiguring it, not entirely realized.

Heat and frost

WW: Why can olive trees endure such intense heat but not frost, and so cannot be cultivated in northern regions?

Olivia: This will change: it will have to. Olives cannot endure frost for in both spiritual and physical terms the frost is a very great and strong being. The fire beings, the salamanders, on the other hand, are very small. Olive trees do not endure these great beings, because their task is to help people gradually to dissolve the stage of earth, whereas the frost helps people to grasp hold of the earth. This is why the frost and its effect is an elemental principle in stark opposition to the olive tree, and one that it cannot endure.

WW: By 'dissolve' do you mean the gradual etherization of the earth in a far-distant future?

Olivia: Yes.

WW: The olive tree is in some ways a tree of the future. Its leaves are as harmonious as the perfect harmony of people in

the fourth post-Atlantean cultural epoch. But now olive trees are burning in Greece, and yesterday you were saying that great forest fires would also prevent some people incarnating in this region. Am I connecting these things in the right way? Can you say anything about this?

Olivia: You're right. Greece is one of the olive tree's classic regions because the ancient Greek saw his ideal form in the olive tree, which did indeed embody it. Now olive trees are burning in Greece because the Greeks of the classical era are no longer present or should no longer incarnate. But this is not the only reason why these olive trees are burning.

WW: How is it for the great olive tree being when whole groves of olives burn down as they have been doing?

Olivia: Of course this isn't good for the olive tree, although it copes better than it would with frost. Fortunately, many of the burned olive trees will sprout again: a germ of life usually survives in the olive's lower portion. Though fire is destructive for the olive tree, it is not such a catastrophe as it is for other species.

Bearer of humanism

WW: Olive trees are among the most common trees on earth, covering a total of 8.6 million hectares. 17.3 million tons of olives are harvested each year. Is it significant for this tree that it appears in such large numbers?

Olivia: The olive tree is aware that it is the bearer of humanism. As long as humanity cannot get beyond the traditions of humanism — which it has not even begun to yet — the olive tree's importance will continue as the human being's I-bearer. So it is not quite correct to see the olive tree as a tree of the

future, for it belongs more to the period of Christianization. As long as Christ works, the olive tree will have a strong future aspect. But in relation to the ideal image of the human being, it has really outlived the peak of its development. The olive tree is still cultivated in such large numbers because human beings cannot — in a spiritual sense — move on yet from the ideal image of humanism.

WW: I said 'tree of the future' because you told me the olive tree enhances the earth's etherization.

Olivia: Indeed it does. In this sense it is a tree of the future; but in relation to human beings it has already passed its prime. In this sense it is an image of the human being's past.

WW: The olive tree plays a major role in cultural history, for instance with the Jews who found it when they reached the promised land. The kings David and Solomon encouraged its cultivation, and for the Greeks in particular it was of outstanding importance, also because its wood was so solid and resilient. How did the Greeks regard olive wood?

Olivia: The solid wood of the wild olive tree enabled the Greeks to make their wooden constructions. The Greeks loved building, and needed scaffolding for their temple sites. Today people tend to overlook this, but most temples could not easily be built without some kind of scaffolding. The Greeks used the enormous stability of wild olive wood for this purpose. The Greek temple could not have been constructed, either, without the model of the olive tree and its harmonious balance of proportions. I mean primarily an inner not outer model. In the temple the inner image of the olive tree comes to expression.

WW: Why did people anoint with oil in olden times?

Olivia: Because oil used to be seen as a kind of concentrated water, and because the viscosity of oil was better suited for preserving the substances contained in it.

WW: Why did the Greeks regard the cultivated olive tree as sacred, and why was it forbidden to fell it?

Olivia: There is both an inner and an outer reason for this. The inner reason was that people could not and were not allowed to fell their own image, feeling this to be sacrilegious. The outer reason was that felling a cultivated olive tree also meant the disappearance of a source of energy. For instance, there were civilizations where the horse was very important, which forbade the slaughter of horses, or where theft of a horse was punishable by death. It was similar in

Greece with the olive. The olive tree was simply vital to sustain the economy.

The ideal human being is a peaceful human being

WW: Why was the olive branch also used as a symbol of peace?

Olivia: This is not very easy to show in outward terms. It is connected with anointing. In Greece both athletes and priests were anointed with oil, a tradition also later preserved in the anointing of kings. The Greeks regarded a good athlete as being on a par with the priests, for he embodied the ideal harmony of human beings. Anointing him with oil also conveyed this

in a physical sense; and because the ideal human being is a peaceful human being, he was given the olive branch as a peace symbol.

WW: Were the victorious athletes crowned with a laurel or olive wreath?

Olivia: Both. In certain circumstances it was a laurel wreath, at other times an olive wreath. In Greece the olive wreath was mostly used because the Greeks had a close connection with the olive. A misinterpretation during the Renaissance led to confusion between the two, so that the laurel wreath became the symbol of victory instead. In former times it was really always an olive wreath.

WW: In Christianity too, the olive branch serves as symbol of

peace. In the Old Testament Noah sends out a dove after the
Flood and it returns with an olive branch in its beak (Gen.,
8–11). What does this image mean?

Olivia: Firstly it means: 'Land ahoy!' The olive tree indicated that
there was more there than just bare rocks with blades of grass,
but a region where life can flourish, where a source of energy
is growing. The olive branch in the dove's beak showed that
they would find something to eat if they went to live in this
region. If necessary you can survive on olives alone.

The garden of Gethsemane

WW: Christ also stays for a while in the garden of Gethsemane
shortly before his crucifixion, and converses with his father.
Do the olive trees have special significance here?

Olivia: Of course. As Pilate expresses this — 'Behold the man!'
— Christ was the ideal human form, the I-bearer embodied
outwardly at that time in the olive tree. The moment Christ
came close to death — when, in the garden of Gethsemane
before his crucifixion, he asked whether the cup might pass
from him — the ideal human being stood together with the
ideal trees in one of the most important circumstances of his
life. His question was whether he would be able to survive
until the crucifixion. That is why the olive tree had to stand
by him. By doing so it represented and sustained the human
being, making possible this situation in the olive grove at night
in which Christ was able to speak with his father. This is very
important!

WW: In Judges (9, 8–9) it says: 'The trees went forth on a time
to anoint a king over them; and they said unto the olive
tree, "Reign thou over us." But the olive tree said unto them,
"Should I leave my fatness, wherewith by me they honour God
and man, and go to be promoted over the trees?"' What is the
meaning of these lines?

Olivia: That the olive tree was aware of its character as server. The
olive tree knew that its fat was a prime means of nutrition for
humanity at the time, whereas a king stands above things and

should not really serve as a staple food. This is why the olive tree asked the other trees about the extent to which they could cope with a king who is at the same time a staple food.

WW: So is the olive tree somehow also a king of the trees?

Olivia: King of the trees of those times, yes. But a king in an inward sense, not outwardly with a purple cloak.

WW: It is interesting that we have here in a certain sense a king of the trees, and that before, from other perspectives, we had the kingdom of horses and the kingdom of lions.

Olivia: And the current king of the trees is the ash. This tree represents the etheric Christ, who is connected with it.

WW: In what way?

Olivia: The ash simply corresponds to Christ. The tree embodies his image.

Islam is inwardly luminous

WW: The olive tree also figures in the Koran, in surah 24:35, 'The Light.' There it says: 'Allah is the Light of the heavens and the earth. The parable of His Light is as if there were a niche, and within it a lamp: the lamp enclosed in glass; the glass as it were a brilliant star; lit from a blessed tree, an olive, neither of the East nor of the West, whose oil is well-nigh luminous, though fire scarce touched it.' Can you say anything about this passage and its significance in relation to the olive tree?

Olivia: Really this should be impressed very forcefully on every conservative or orthodox Islamist, for it definitely shows that true Islam is not a conquering religion, neither in the East nor in the West, but is inwardly luminous. This relates among other things to the wonderful colour of olive oil, which is luminous in the same way as the real luminosity of Islam. The archangel Gabriel dictated the surahs to Muhammad; this is known, and all agree about it. The archangel Gabriel emphasizes that spiritual warmth should not be kindled through external combustion but through transformation of an inner quality: the ideal human image which olive oil already hints at, the outpouring as it were of this image, which really no longer needs any external flame. At the same time this is an indication that the practice of religion should take place within, not externally.

The harmonious human being and love

WW: In the Odyssey (song 23, lines 190–201), Odysseus has a shady olive tree whose trunk is as thick as a pillar. He builds a marriage bed from it and the bed's single foot is the root of the olive. The bed is firmly anchored in the olive tree root and is seen as one of the love secrets between Odysseus and his wife Penelope. What secret of love does this relate to?

Olivia: It shows that love between people can really only be lasting when it grows through time. At the same time this is connected also with a reversal in the sense that the root corresponds to the human being's crown. This means that love is only true if it draws its powers from the world of spirit and is firmly rooted in human hearts. And this also invokes the wholly harmonious human being, who is reflected in the harmonious olive tree.

WW: What human quality corresponds to the olive tree?

Olivia: The power of human harmony, the power for inner harmony; the striving to bring everything into proper, harmonious proportion.

Contributing Photographers and Artists

Books to challenge  *your perception of reality*

A message from Clairview

We are an independent publishing company with a focus on cutting-edge, non-fiction books. Our innovative list covers current affairs and politics, health, the arts, history, science and spirituality. But regardless of subject, our books have a common link: they all question conventional thinking, dogmas and received wisdom.

Despite being a small company, our list features some big names, such as Booker Prize winner Ben Okri, literary giant Gore Vidal, world leader Mikhail Gorbachev, modern artist Joseph Beuys and natural childbirth pioneer Michel Odent.

So, check out our full catalogue online at
www.clairviewbooks.com
and join our emailing list for news on new titles.

office@clairviewbooks.com

CLAIRVIEW